STAR WARS®

CLONE WARS
ADVENTURES
VOLUME 5

designers
Darin Fabrick and Josh Elliott

assistant editor
Dave Marshall

editor
Jeremy Barlow

publisher
Mike Richardson

special thanks to Sue Rostoni, Leland Chee,
and Amy Gary at Lucas Licensing

talk about this book online at: www.darkhorse.com/community/boards

The events in this story take place
just before and during the events in
Star Wars: Episode III *Revenge of the Sith*

Advertising Sales: (503) 652-8815 x370
Comic Shop Locator Service: (888) 266-4226
www.darkhorse.com
www.starwars.com

5 7 9 10 8 6 4

STAR WARS: CLONE WARS ADVENTURES Volume 5, April 2006. Published
by Dark Horse Comics, Inc., 10956 SE Main Street, Milwaukie, OR 97222. Star Wars
©2006 Lucasfilm Ltd. & ™. All rights reserved. Used under authorization. Text and
illustrations for Star Wars are © 2006 Lucasfilm Ltd. Dark Horse Books™ is a trademark
of Dark Horse Comics, Inc. All rights reserved. No portion of this publication may be
reproduced or transmitted, in any form or by any means, without the express written
permission of Dark Horse Comics, Inc. Names, characters, places, and incidents
featured in this publication either are the product of the author's imagination or are
used fictiously. Any resemblance to actual persons (living or dead), events, institutions,
or locales, without satiric intent, is coincidental. PRINTED IN CHINA

STAR WARS

CLONE WARS ADVENTURES

VOLUME 5

WHAT GOES UP . . .

script and art The Fillbach Brothers

colors Lee Evandon

BAILED OUT

script Justin Lambros

art The Fillbach Brothers

colors David Nestelle

HEROES ON BOTH SIDES

script Chris Avellone

art Stewart McKenney

colors Dan Jackson

ORDER OF OUTCASTS

script Matt Jacobs

art The Fillbach Brothers

colors Lee Evandon

lettering
Michael David Thomas

cover
The Fillbach Brothers and Dan Jackson

Dark Horse Books™

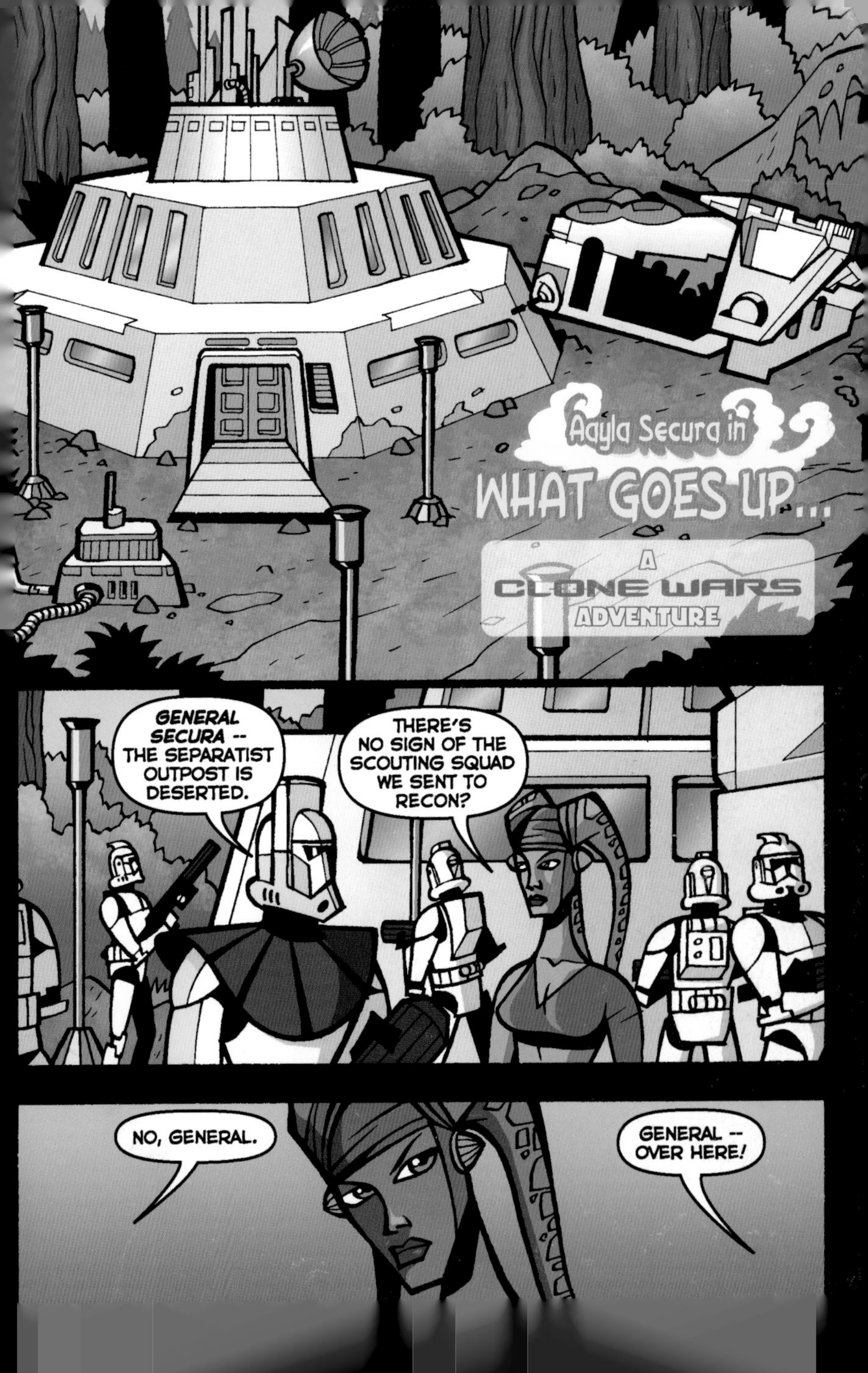
Aayla Secura in
WHAT GOES UP...
A CLONE WARS ADVENTURE
GENERAL SECURA -- THE SEPARATIST OUTPOST IS DESERTED.
THERE'S NO SIGN OF THE SCOUTING SQUAD WE SENT TO RECON?
NO, GENERAL.
GENERAL -- OVER HERE!

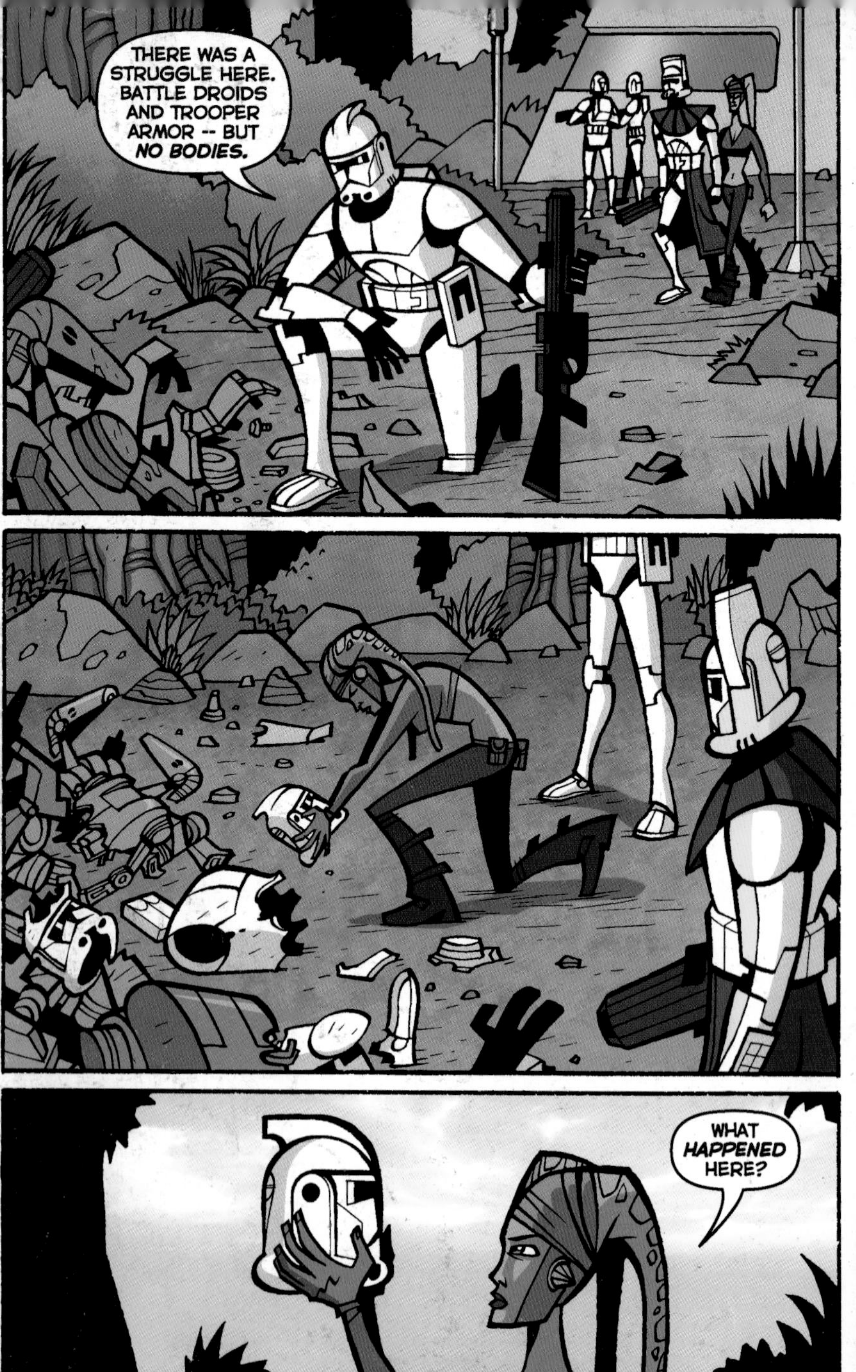
THERE WAS A STRUGGLE HERE. BATTLE DROIDS AND TROOPER ARMOR -- BUT NO BODIES.
WHAT HAPPENED HERE?

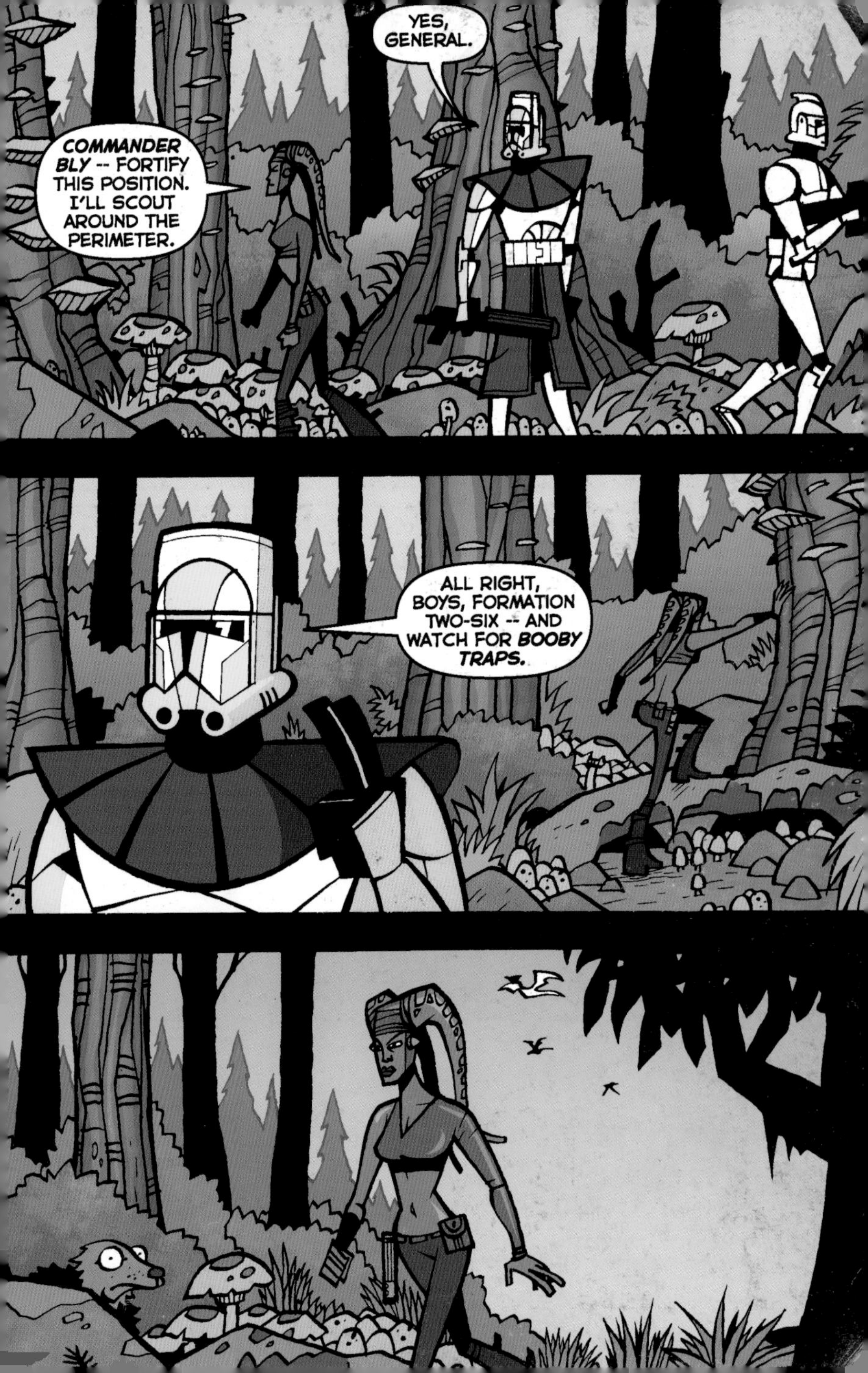
COMMANDER BLY -- FORTIFY THIS POSITION. I'LL SCOUT AROUND THE PERIMETER.
YES, GENERAL.
ALL RIGHT, BOYS, FORMATION TWO-SIX -- AND WATCH FOR BOOBY TRAPS.

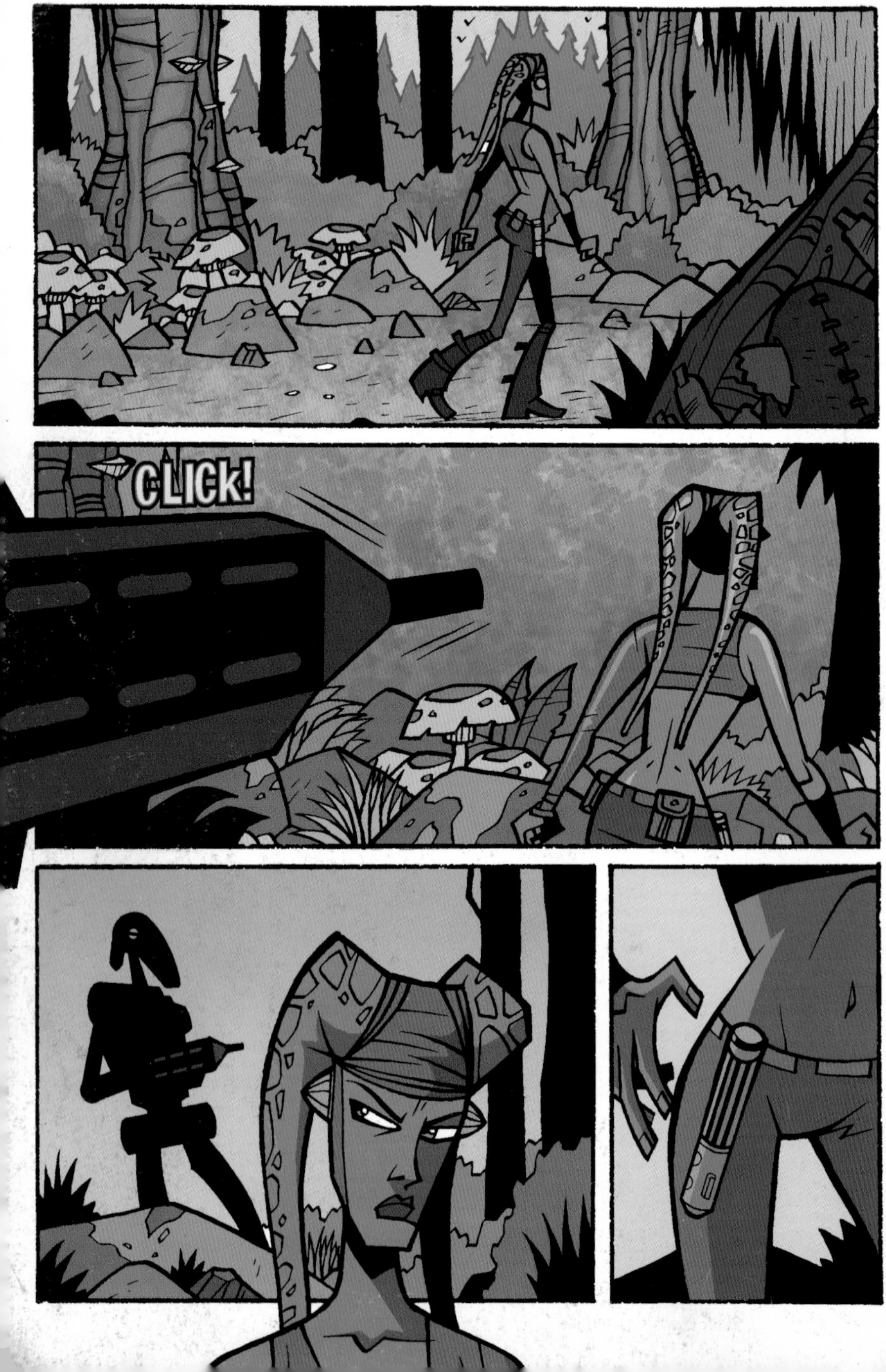
CLICK!

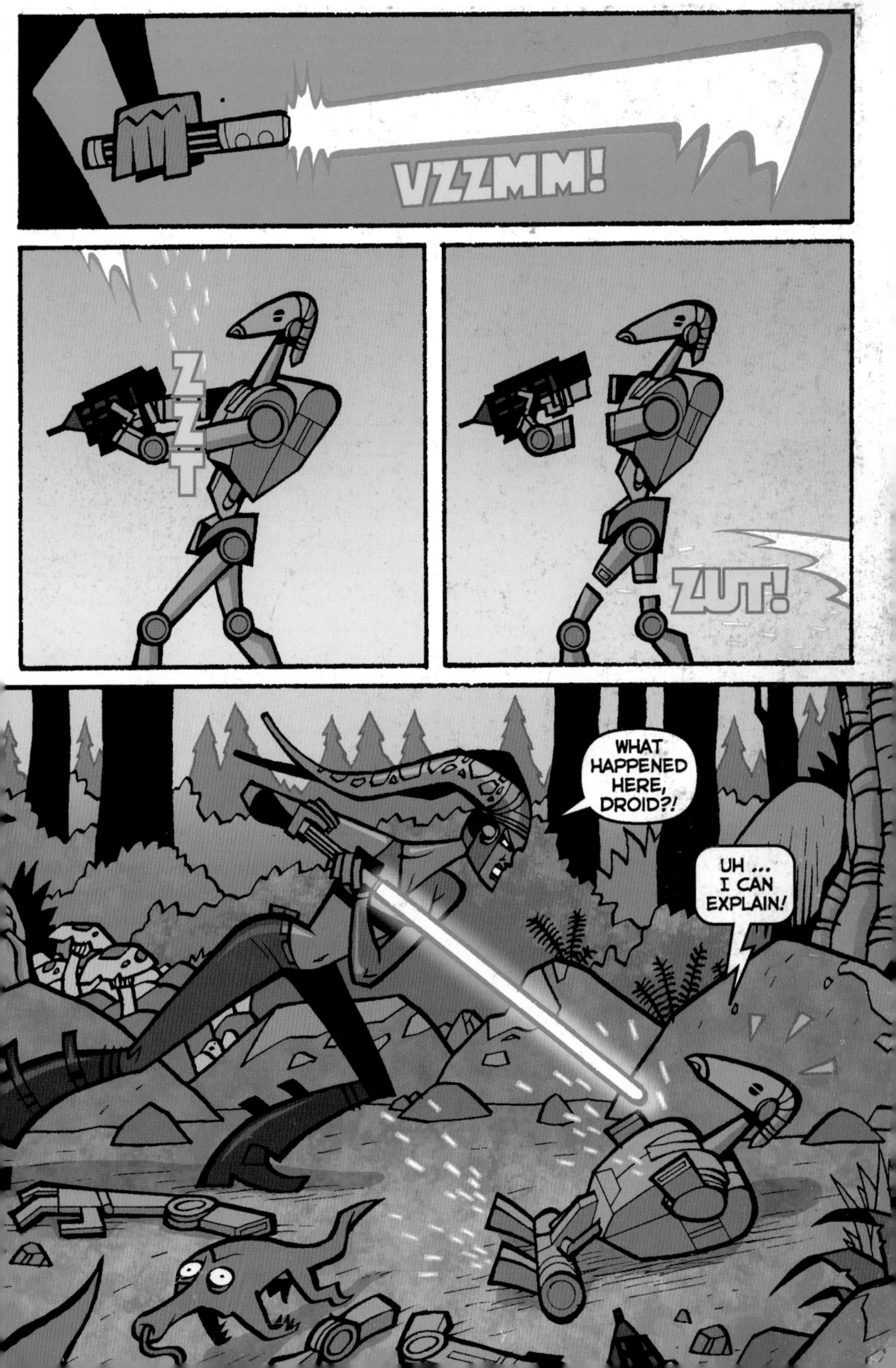
VZZMM!
ZZZT
ZUT!
WHAT HAPPENED HERE, DROID?!
UH ... I CAN EXPLAIN!

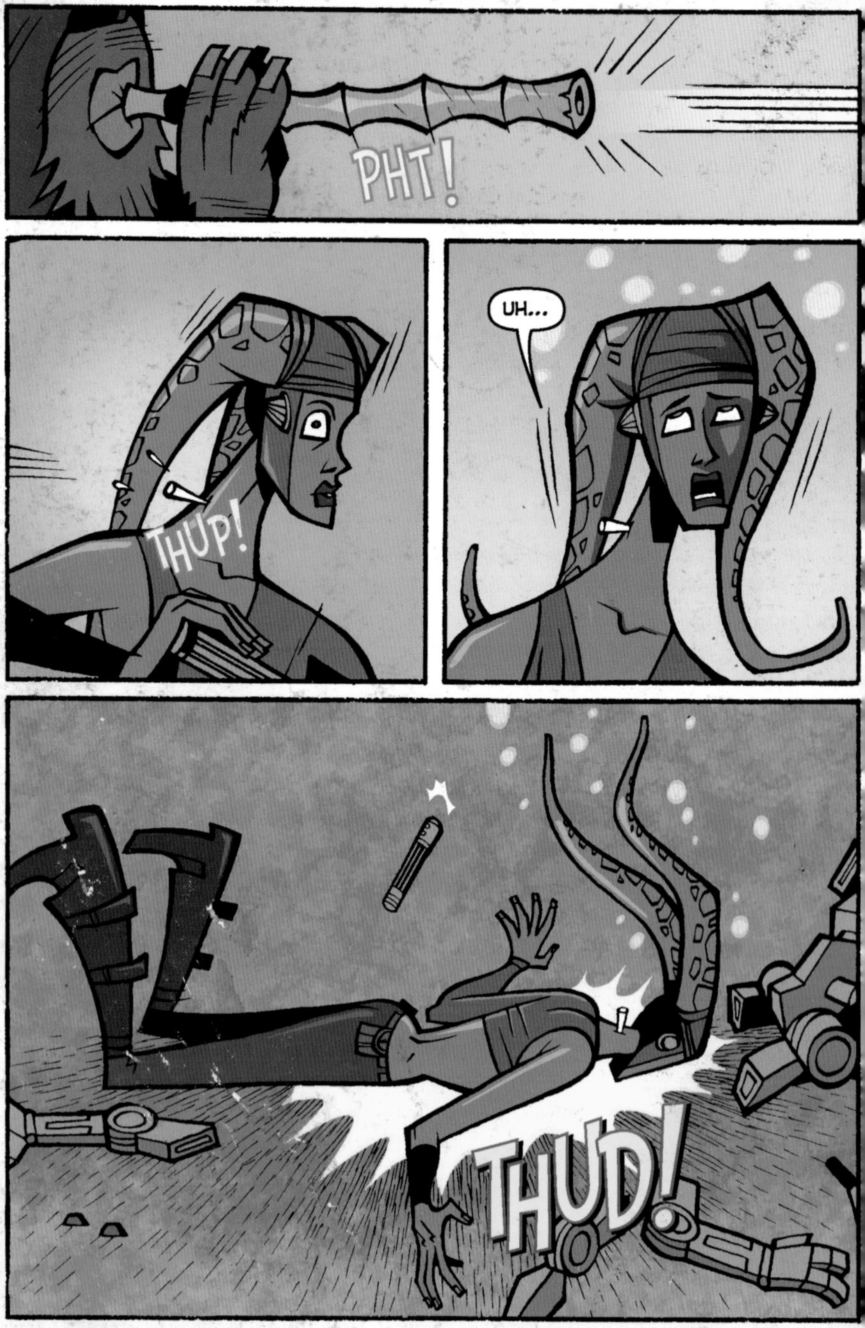
PHT!
THUP!
UH...
THUD!

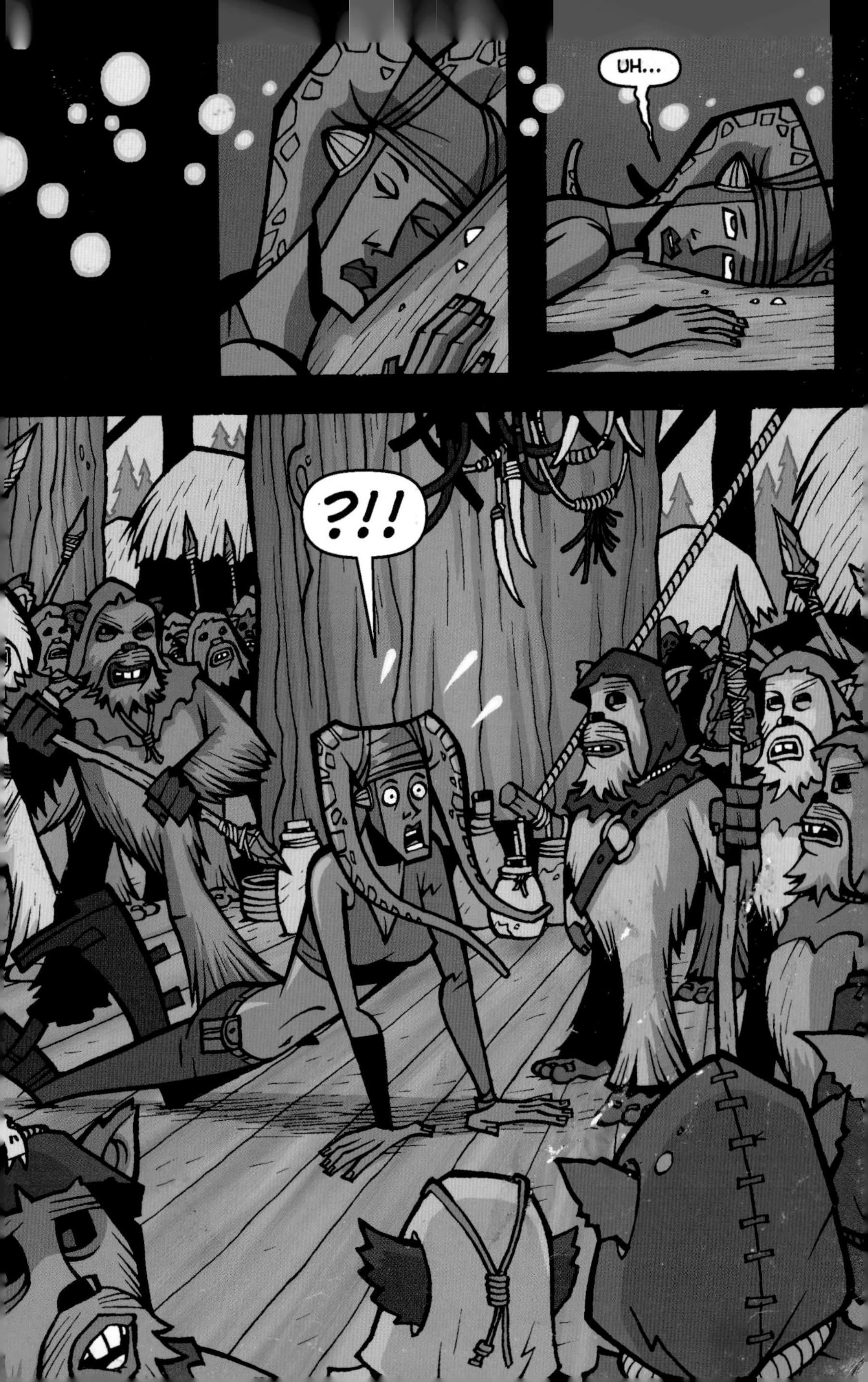
UH...
?!!

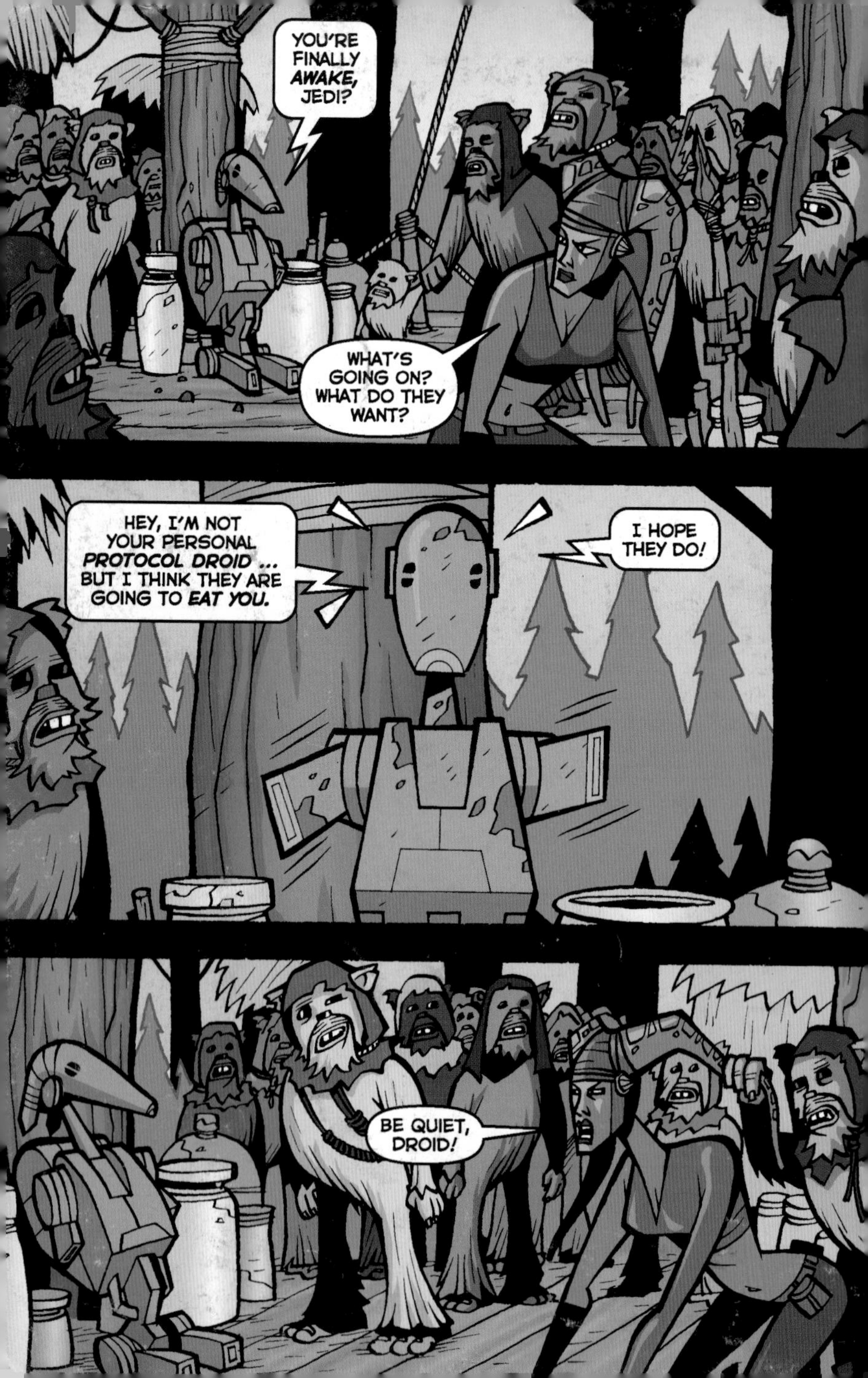
YOU'RE FINALLY AWAKE, JEDI?
WHAT'S GOING ON? WHAT DO THEY WANT?
HEY, I'M NOT YOUR PERSONAL PROTOCOL DROID ... BUT I THINK THEY ARE GOING TO EAT YOU.
I HOPE THEY DO!
BE QUIET, DROID!

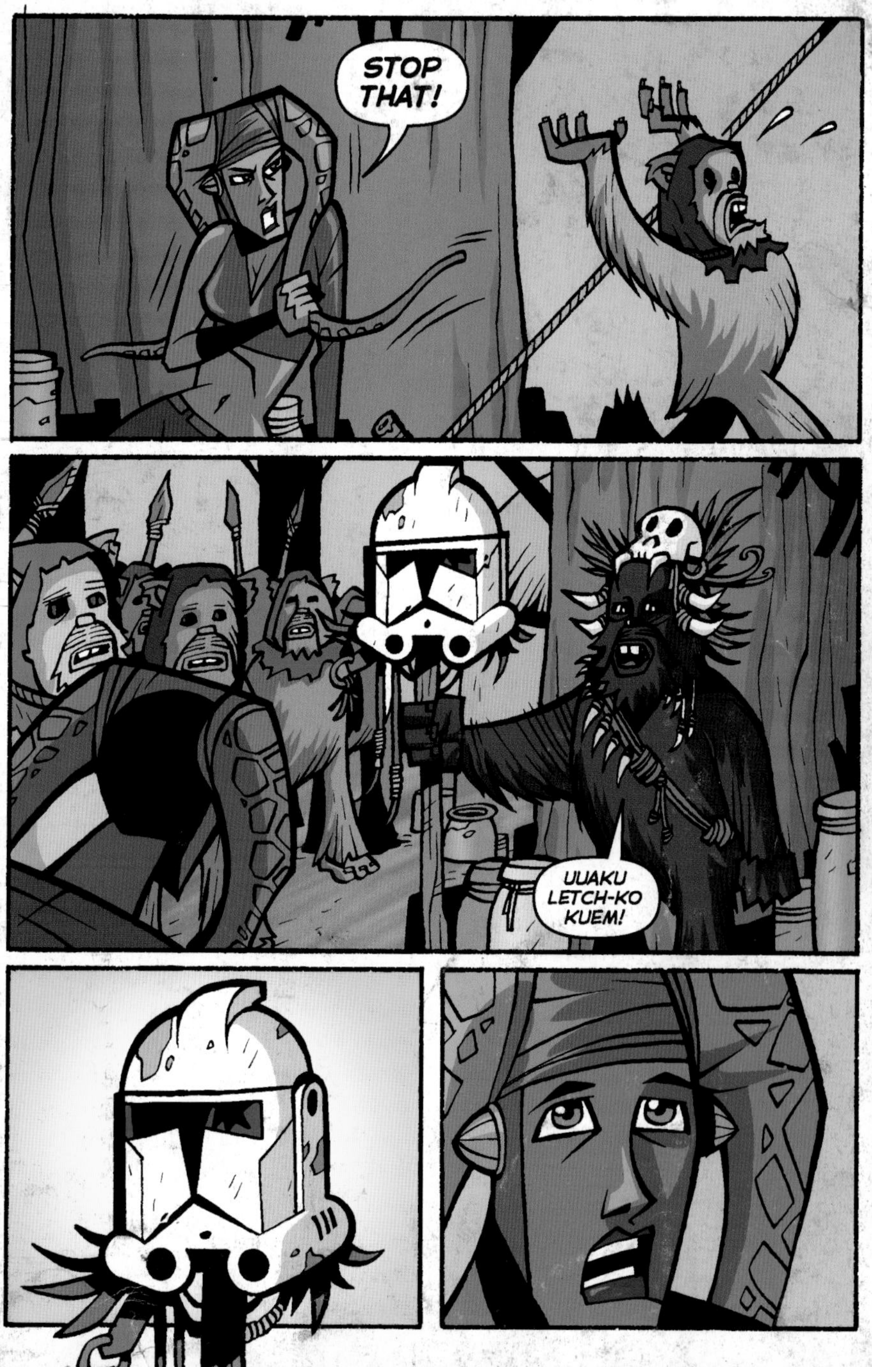
STOP THAT!
UUAKU LETCH-KO KUEM!

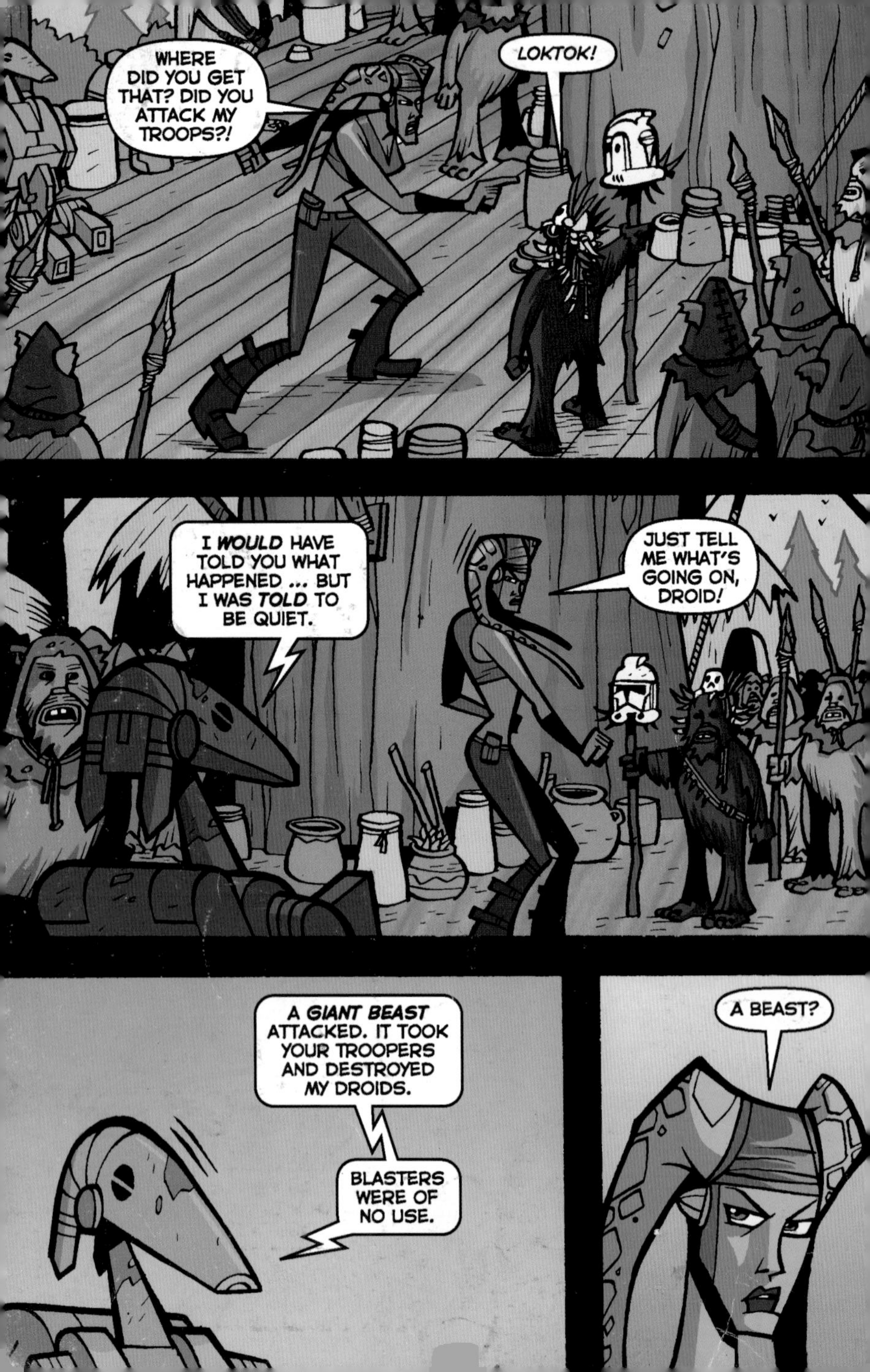
WHERE DID YOU GET THAT? DID YOU ATTACK MY TROOPS?!
LOKTOK!
I *WOULD* HAVE TOLD YOU WHAT HAPPENED ... BUT I WAS *TOLD* TO BE QUIET.
JUST TELL ME WHAT'S GOING ON, DROID!
A *GIANT BEAST* ATTACKED. IT TOOK YOUR TROOPERS AND DESTROYED MY DROIDS.
BLASTERS WERE OF NO USE.
A BEAST?

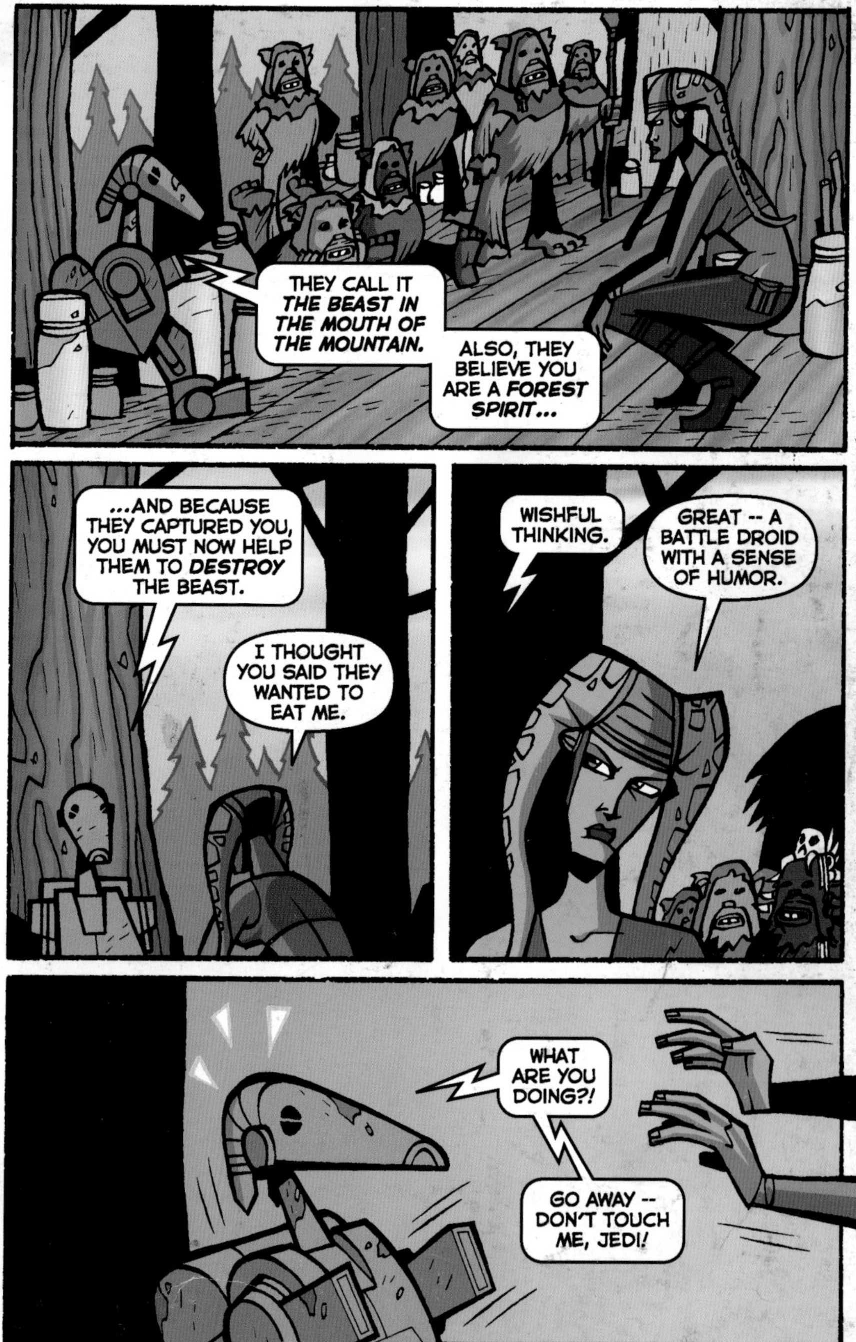
THEY CALL IT *THE BEAST IN THE MOUTH OF THE MOUNTAIN.*
ALSO, THEY BELIEVE YOU ARE A *FOREST SPIRIT*...
...AND BECAUSE THEY CAPTURED YOU, YOU MUST NOW HELP THEM TO *DESTROY* THE BEAST.
I THOUGHT YOU SAID THEY WANTED TO EAT ME.
WISHFUL THINKING.
GREAT -- A BATTLE DROID WITH A SENSE OF HUMOR.
WHAT ARE YOU DOING?!
GO AWAY -- DON'T TOUCH ME, JEDI!

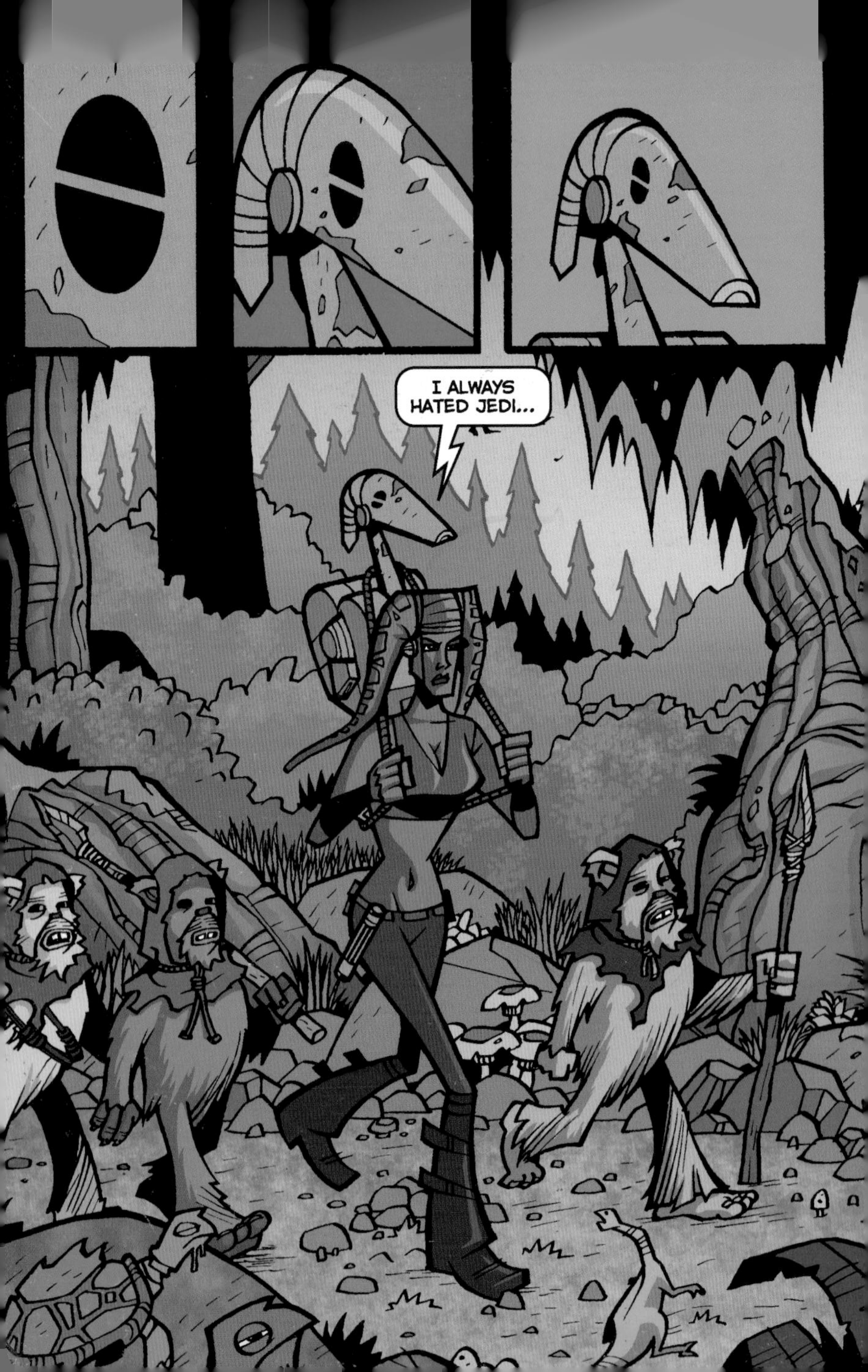
I ALWAYS HATED JEDI...

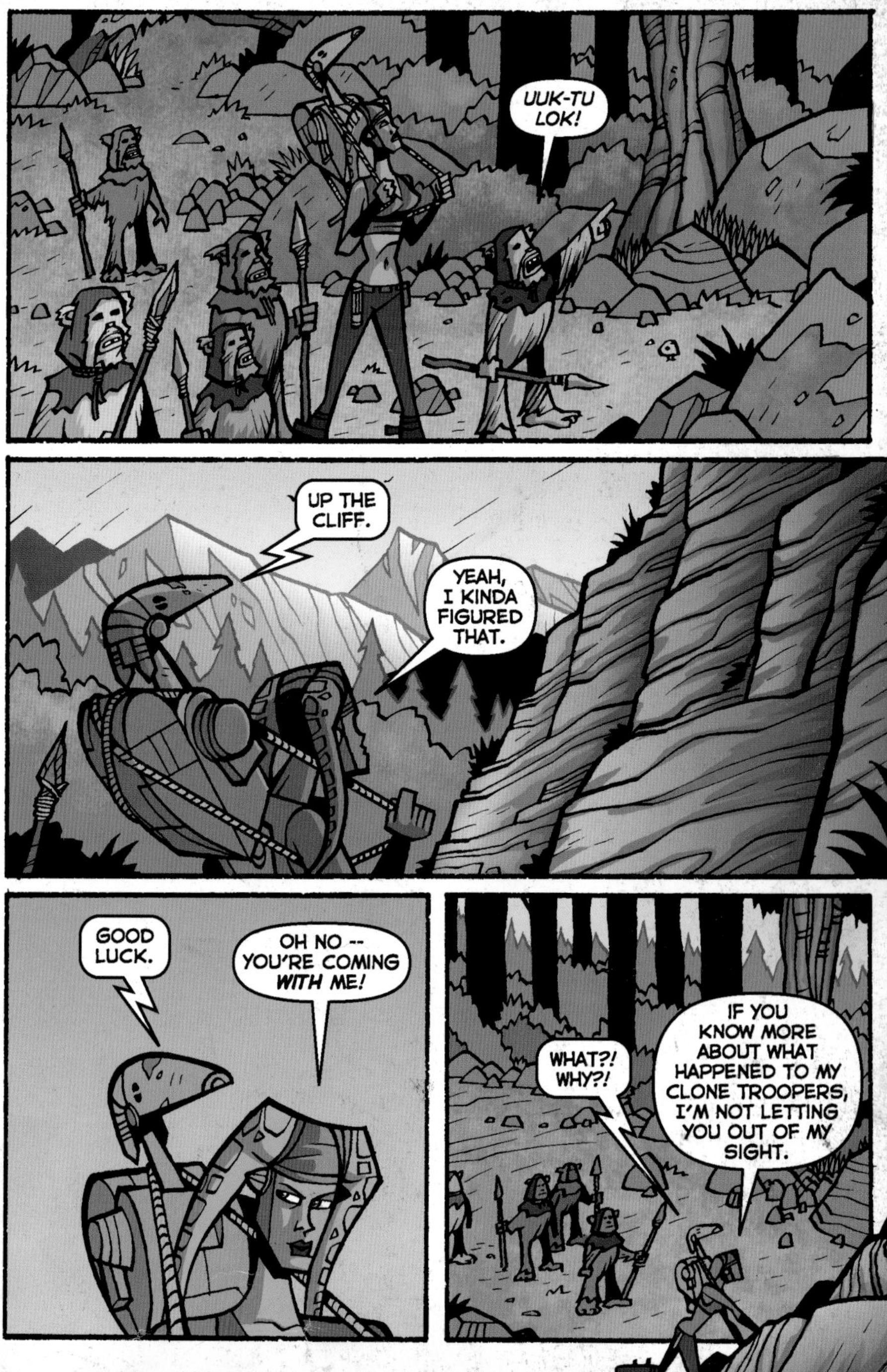
UUK-TU LOK!
UP THE CLIFF.
YEAH, I KINDA FIGURED THAT.
GOOD LUCK.
OH NO -- YOU'RE COMING *WITH ME!*
WHAT?! WHY?!
IF YOU KNOW MORE ABOUT WHAT HAPPENED TO MY CLONE TROOPERS, I'M NOT LETTING YOU OUT OF MY SIGHT.

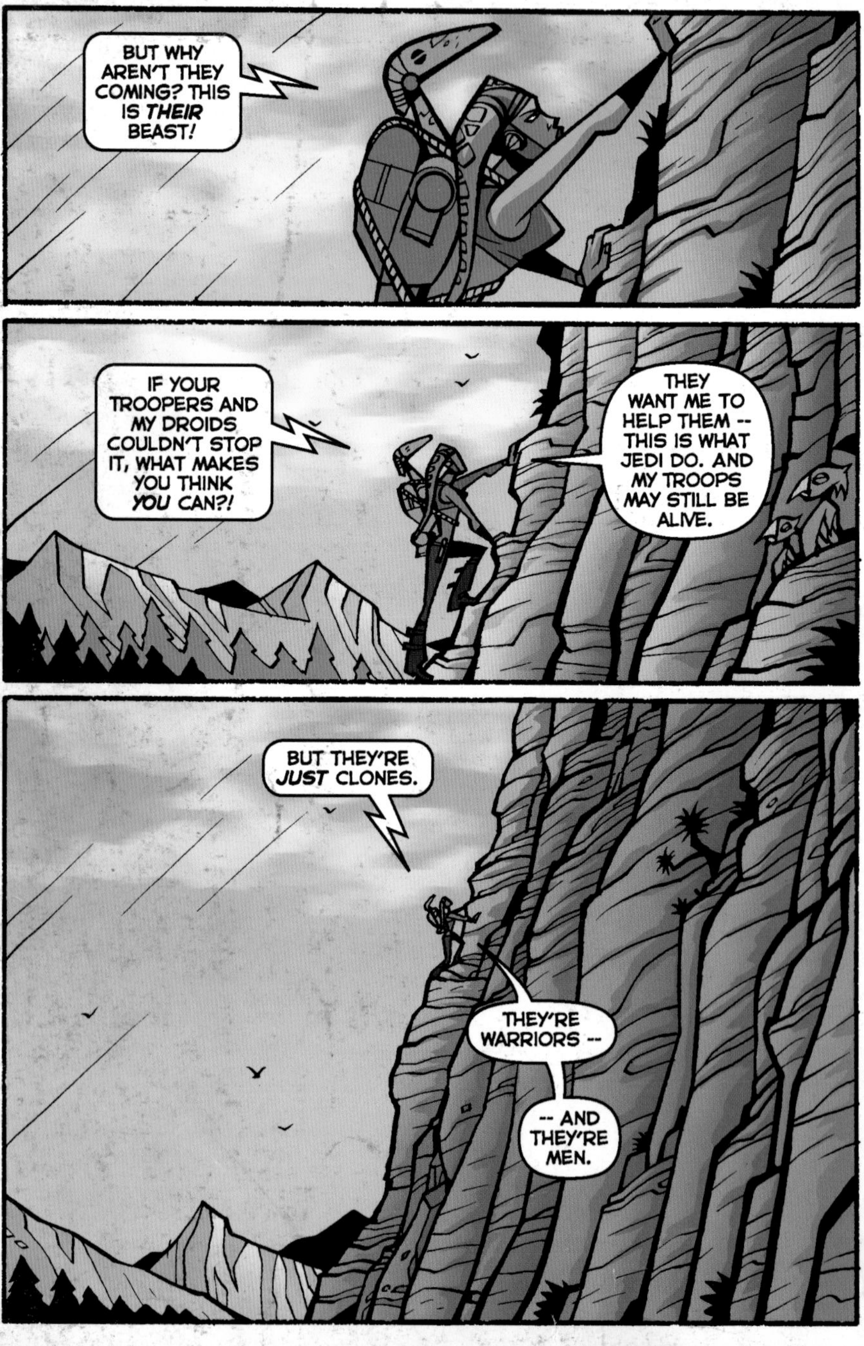
BUT WHY AREN'T THEY COMING? THIS IS *THEIR* BEAST!
IF YOUR TROOPERS AND MY DROIDS COULDN'T STOP IT, WHAT MAKES YOU THINK *YOU* CAN?!
THEY WANT ME TO HELP THEM -- THIS IS WHAT JEDI DO. AND MY TROOPS MAY STILL BE ALIVE.
BUT THEY'RE *JUST* CLONES.
THEY'RE WARRIORS --
-- AND THEY'RE MEN.

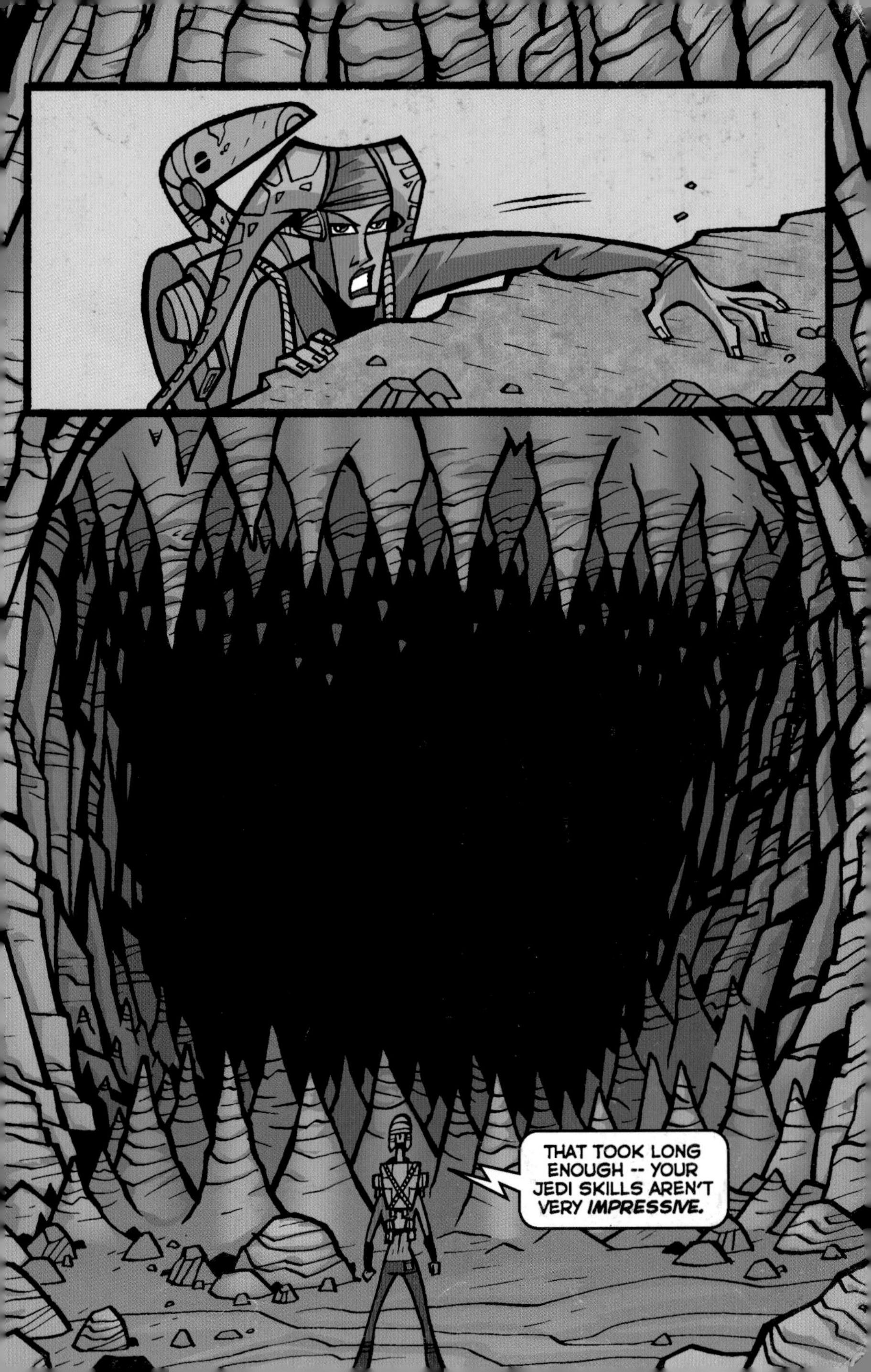
THAT TOOK LONG ENOUGH -- YOUR JEDI SKILLS AREN'T VERY IMPRESSIVE.

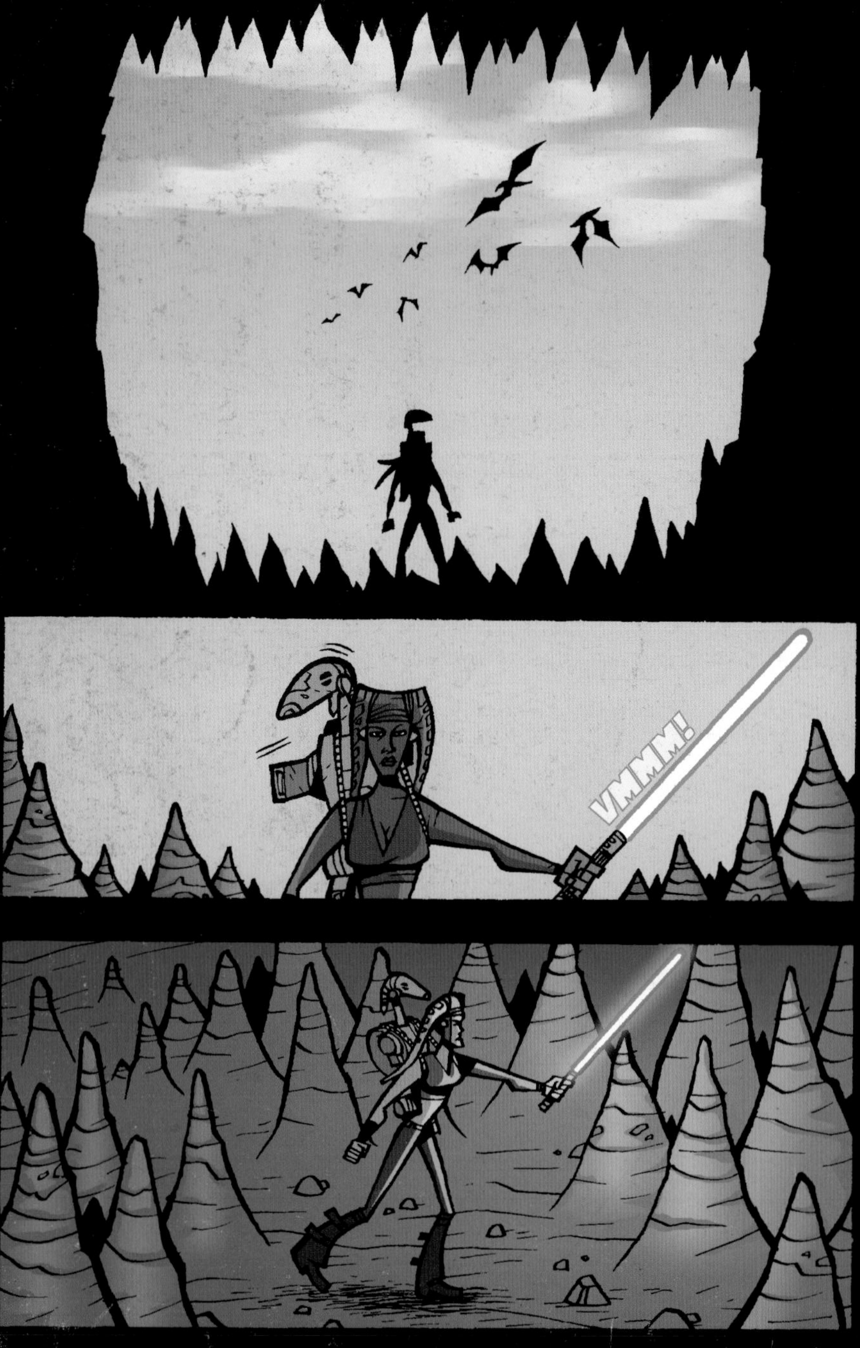
VMMM!

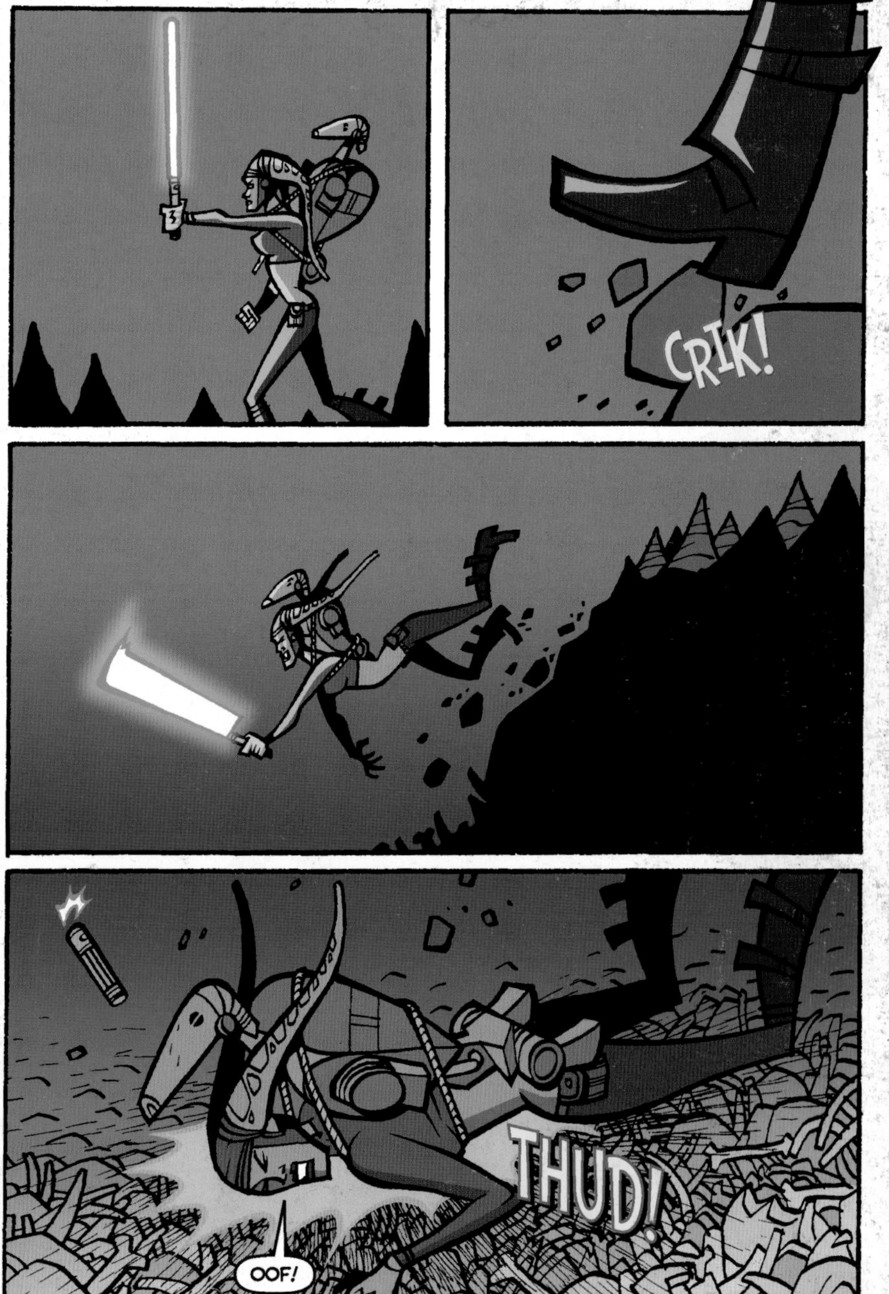
CRIK!
THUD!
OOF!

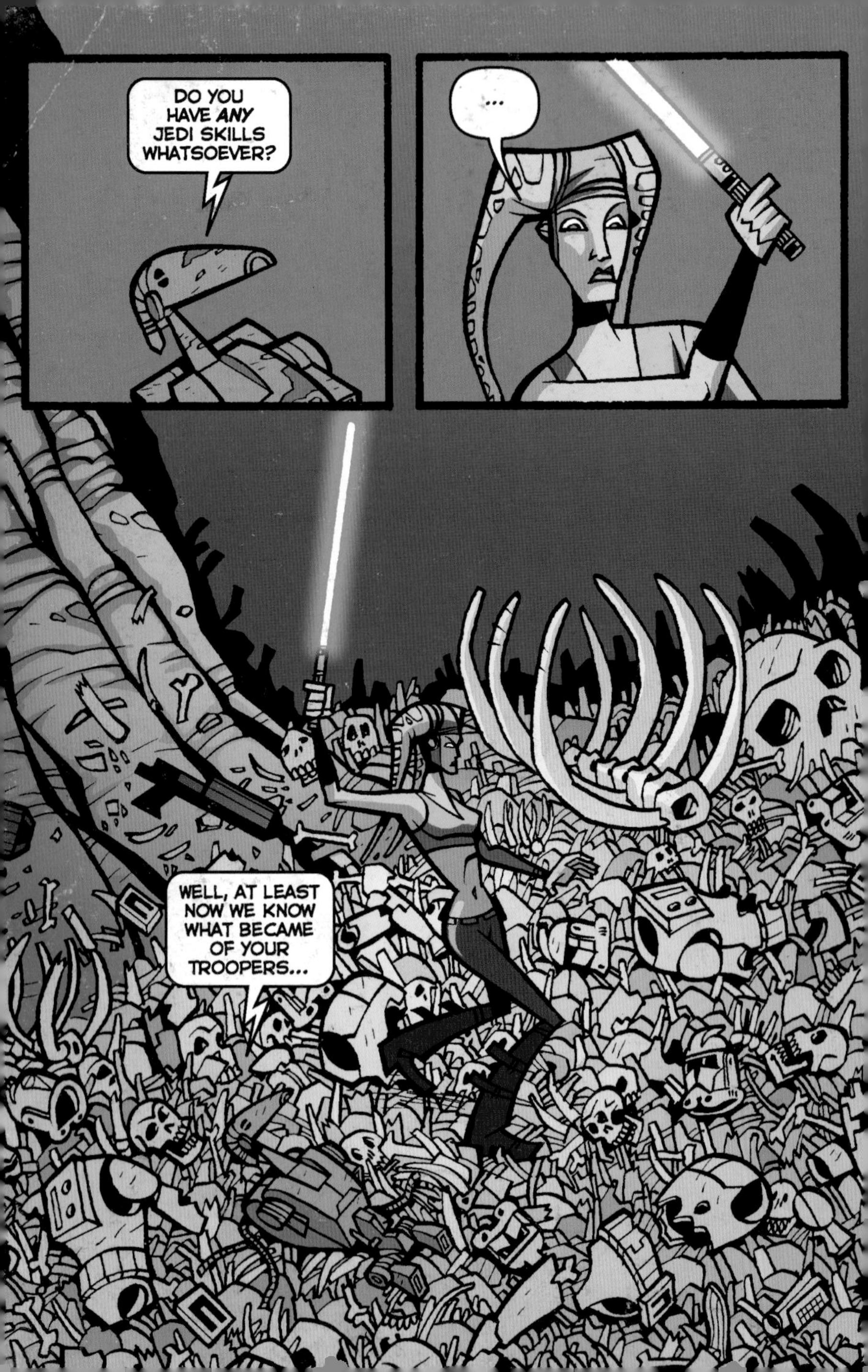
DO YOU HAVE *ANY* JEDI SKILLS WHATSOEVER?
...
WELL, AT LEAST NOW WE KNOW WHAT BECAME OF YOUR TROOPERS...

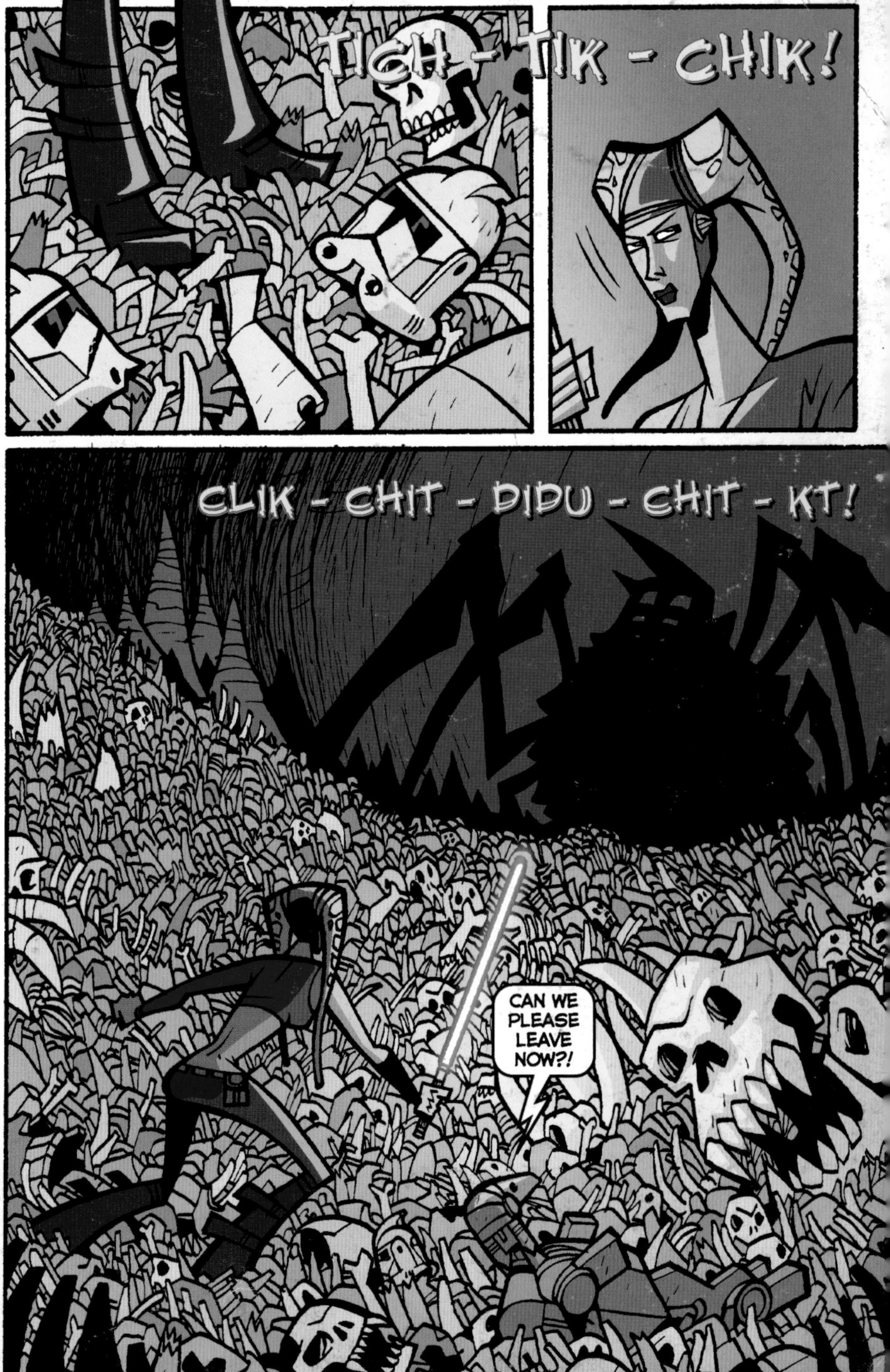
TICH - TIK - CHIK!
CLIK - CHIT - DIDU - CHIT - KT!
CAN WE PLEASE LEAVE NOW?!

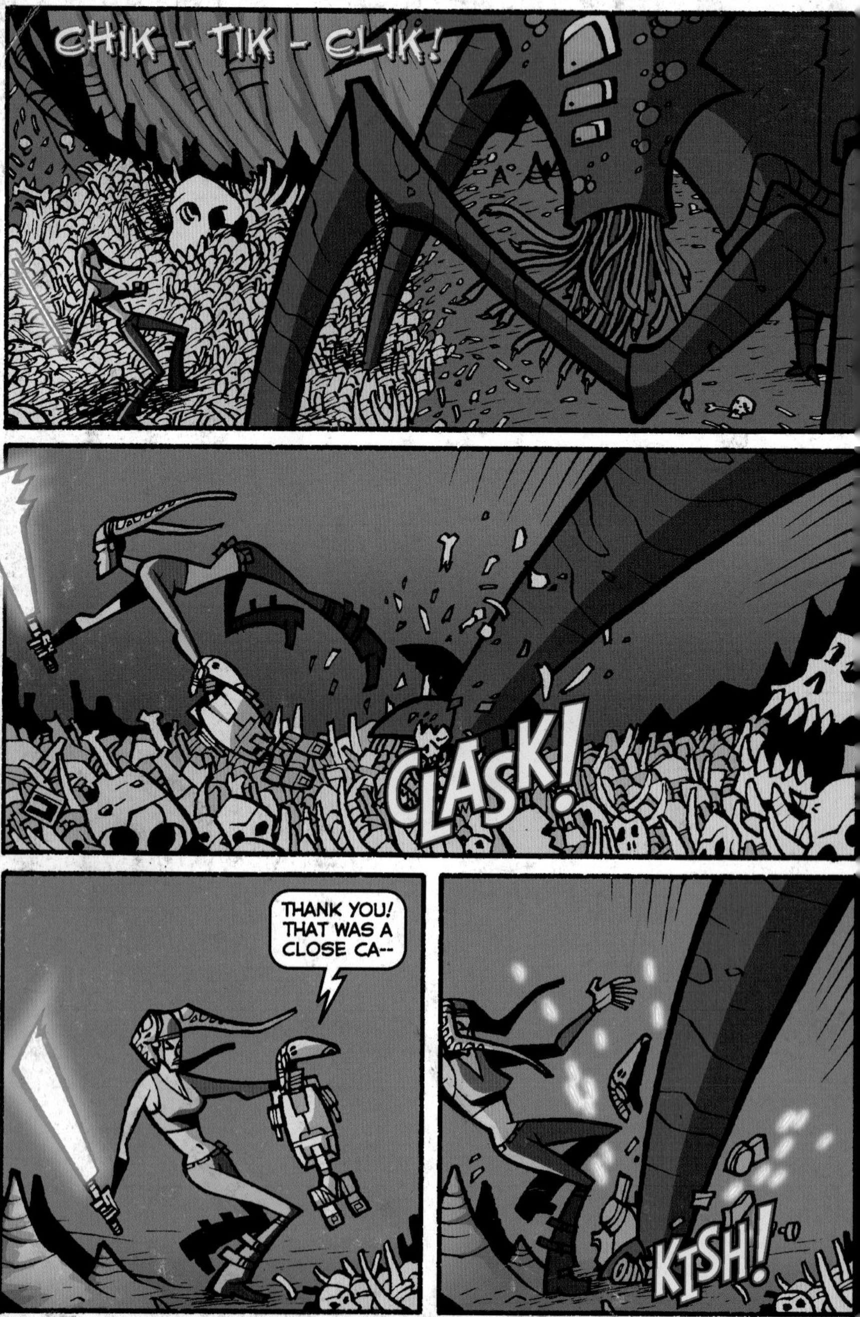
CHIK - TIK - CLIK!
CLASK!
THANK YOU! THAT WAS A CLOSE CA--
KISH!

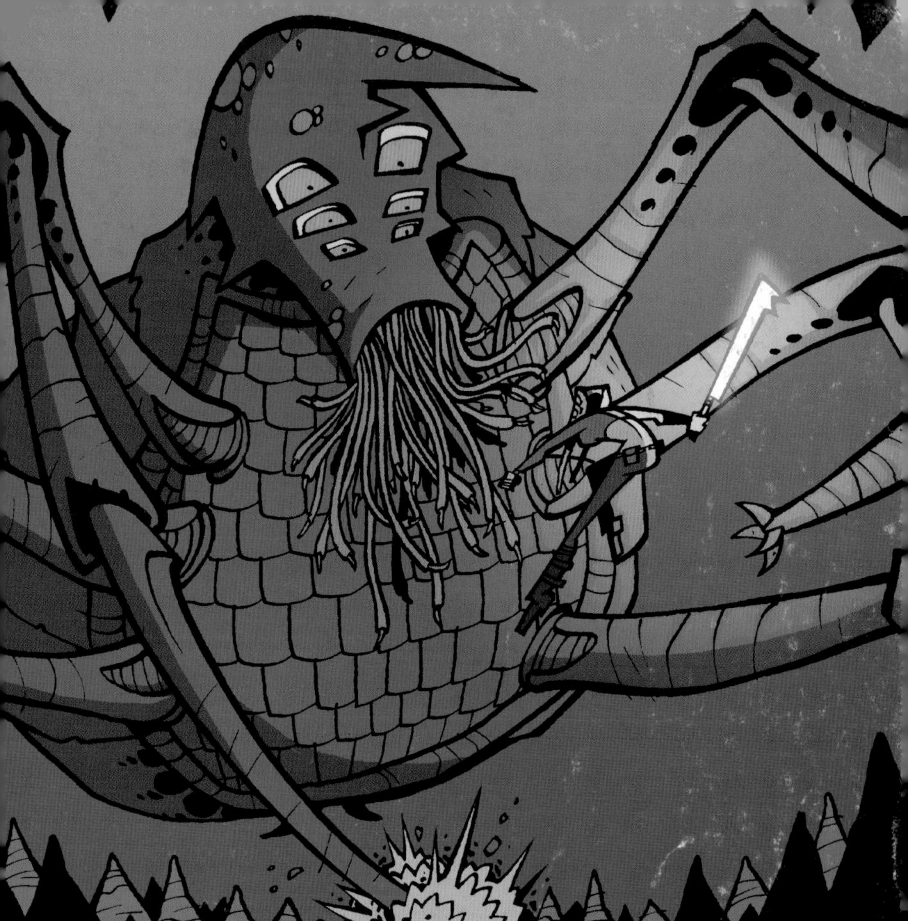

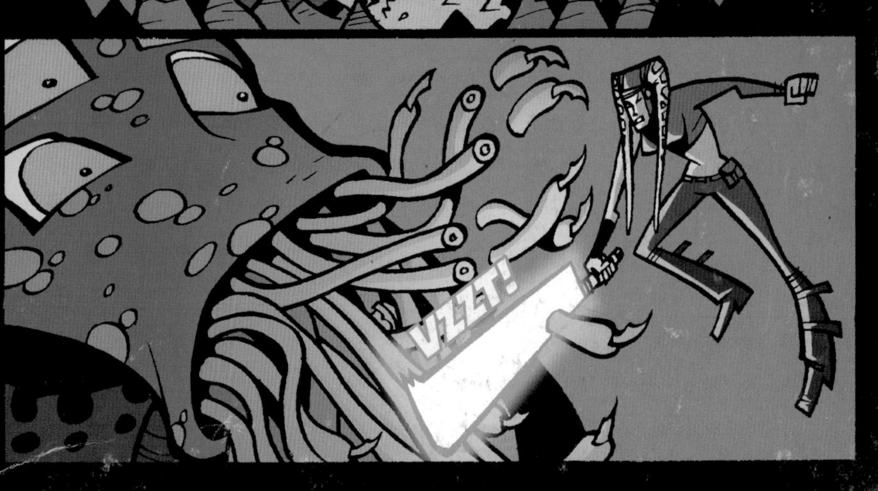
VZZZT!

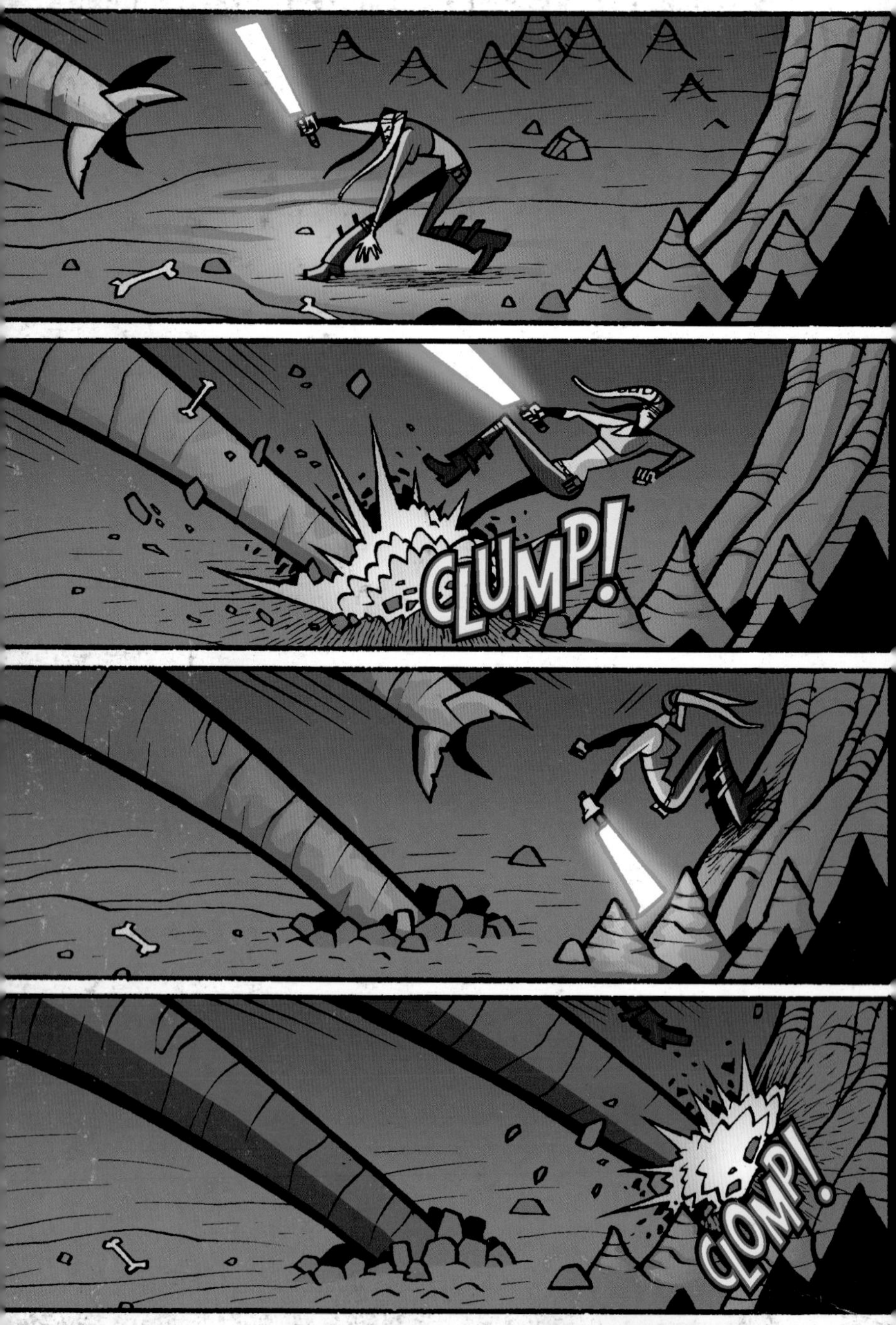
CLUMP!
CLOMP!

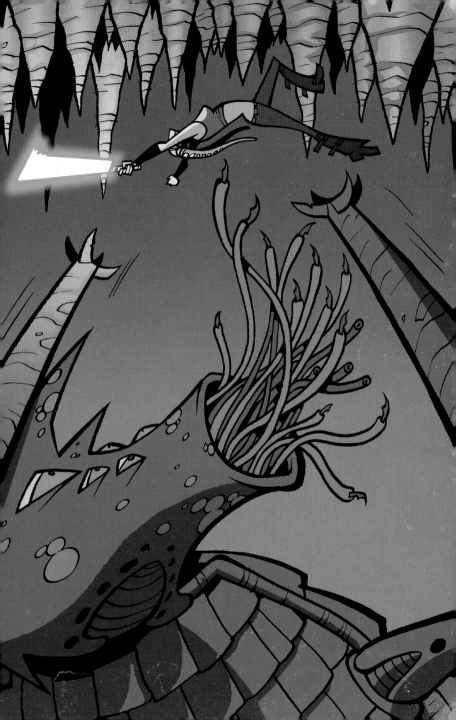

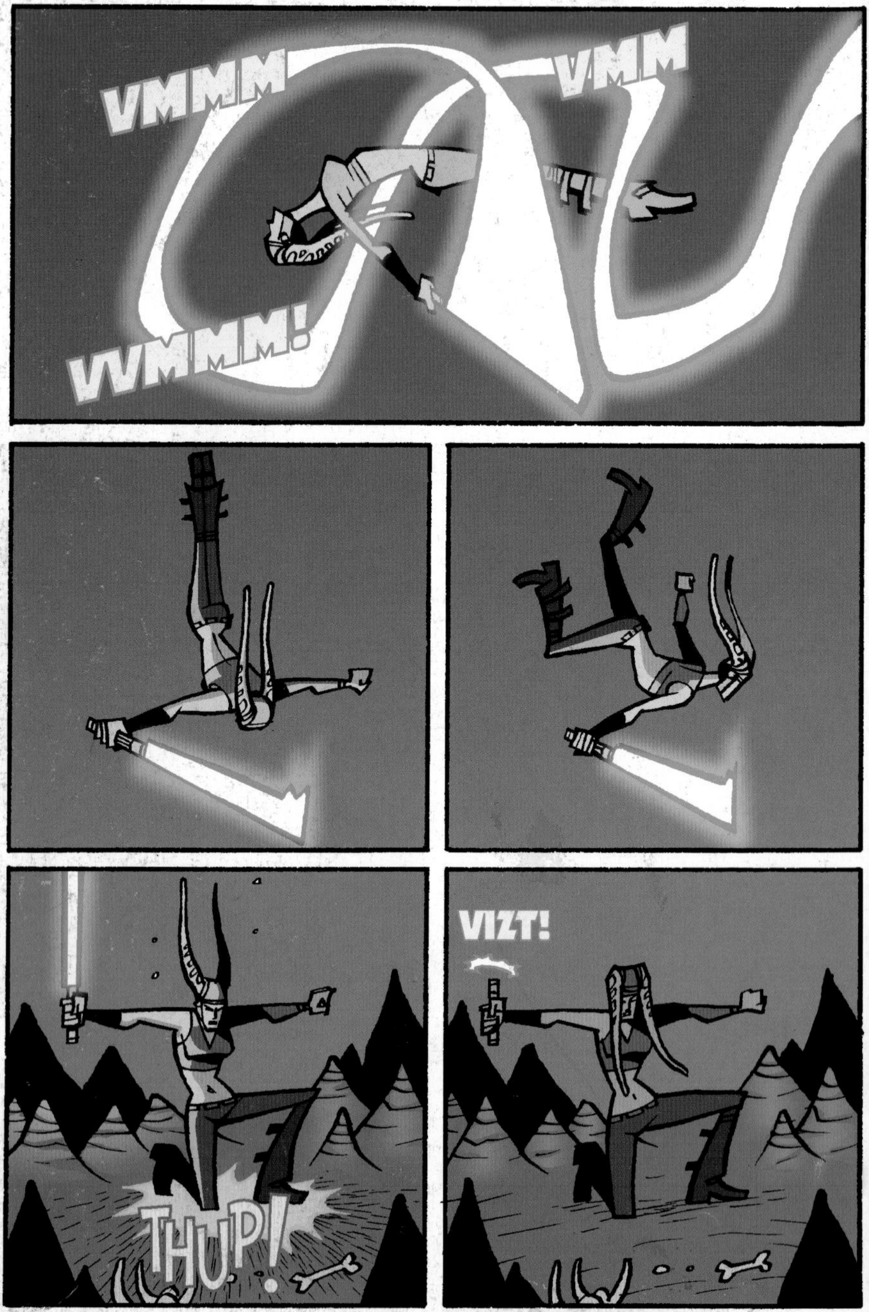
VMMM
VMM
VVMMM!
THUP!
VIZT!

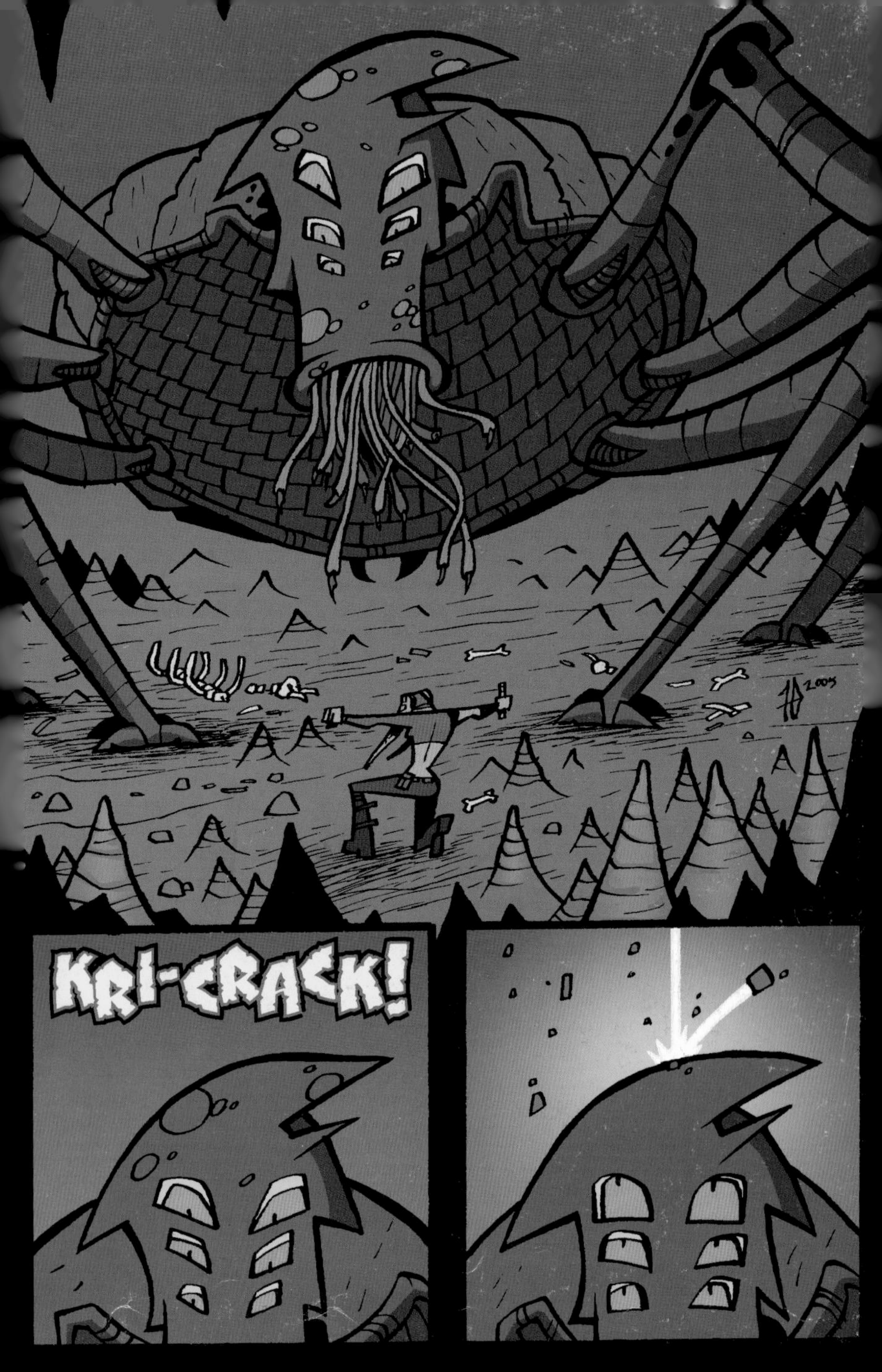
KRI-CRACK!

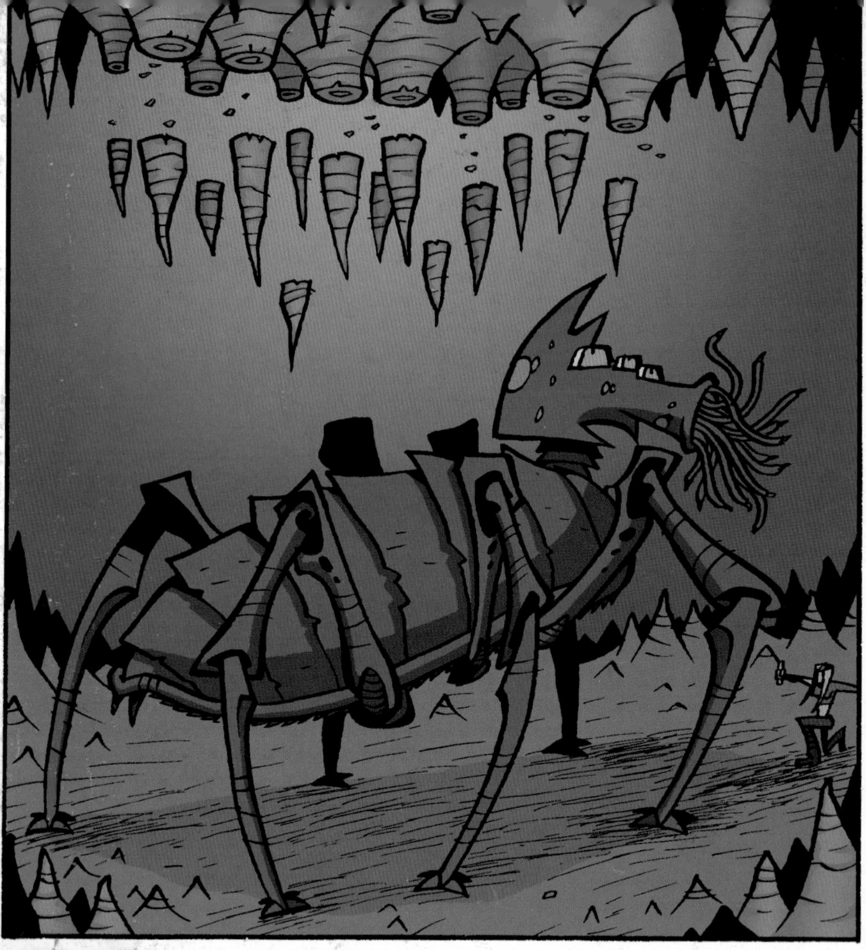

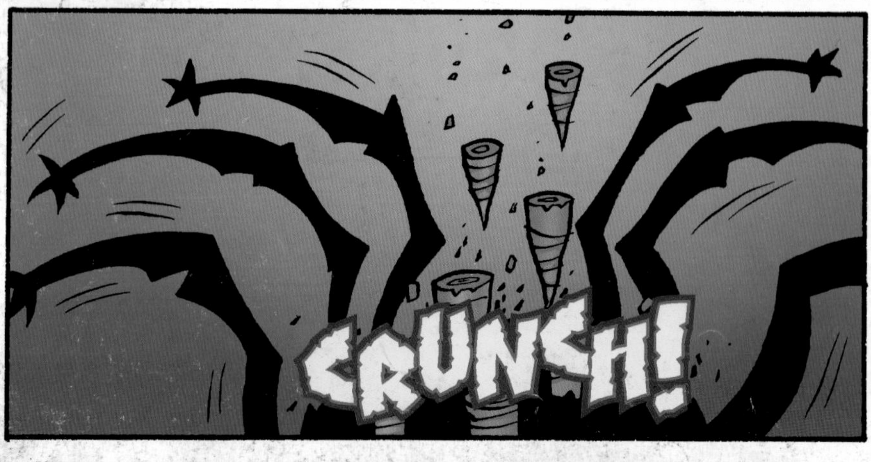
CRUNCH!

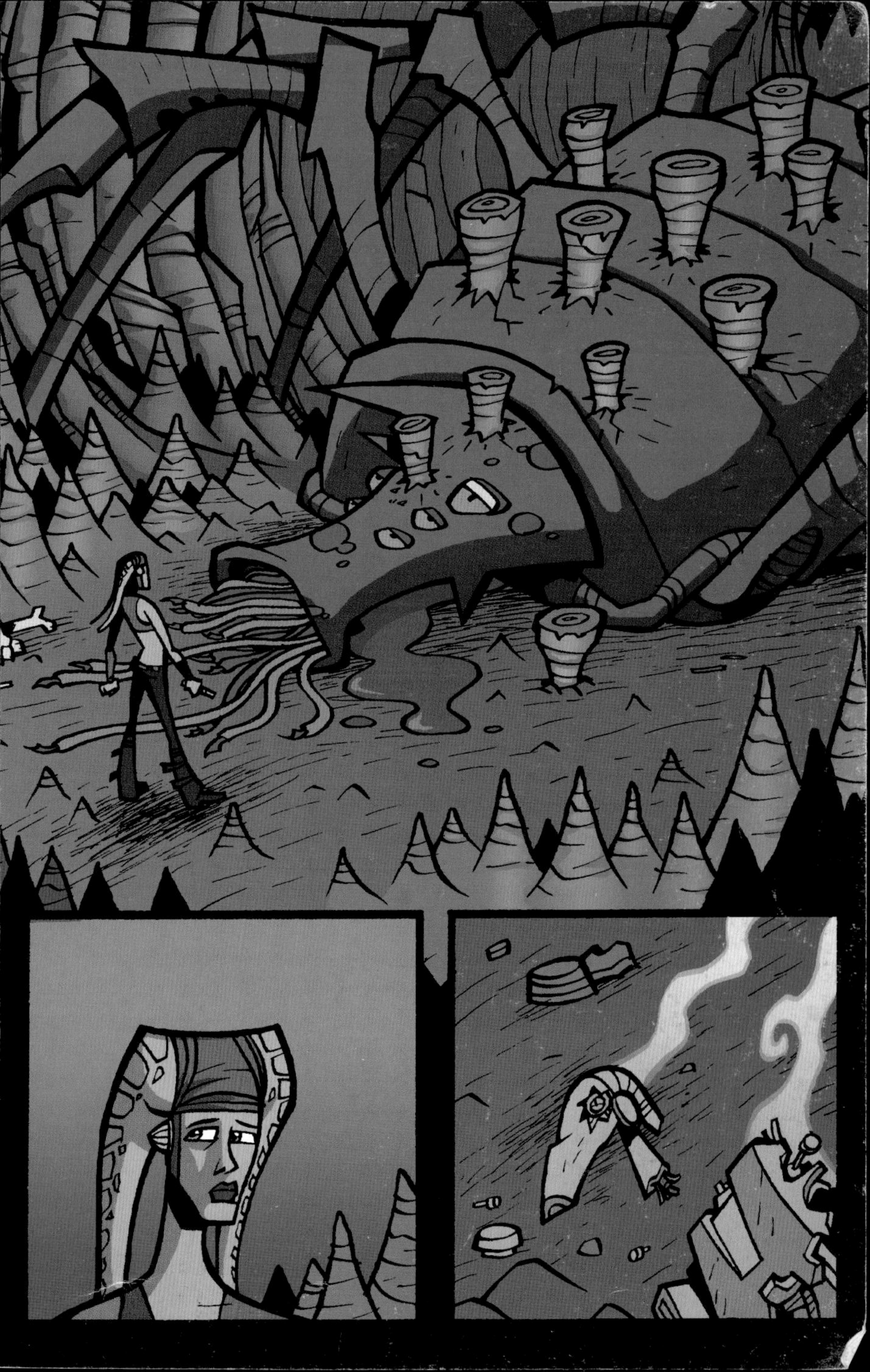

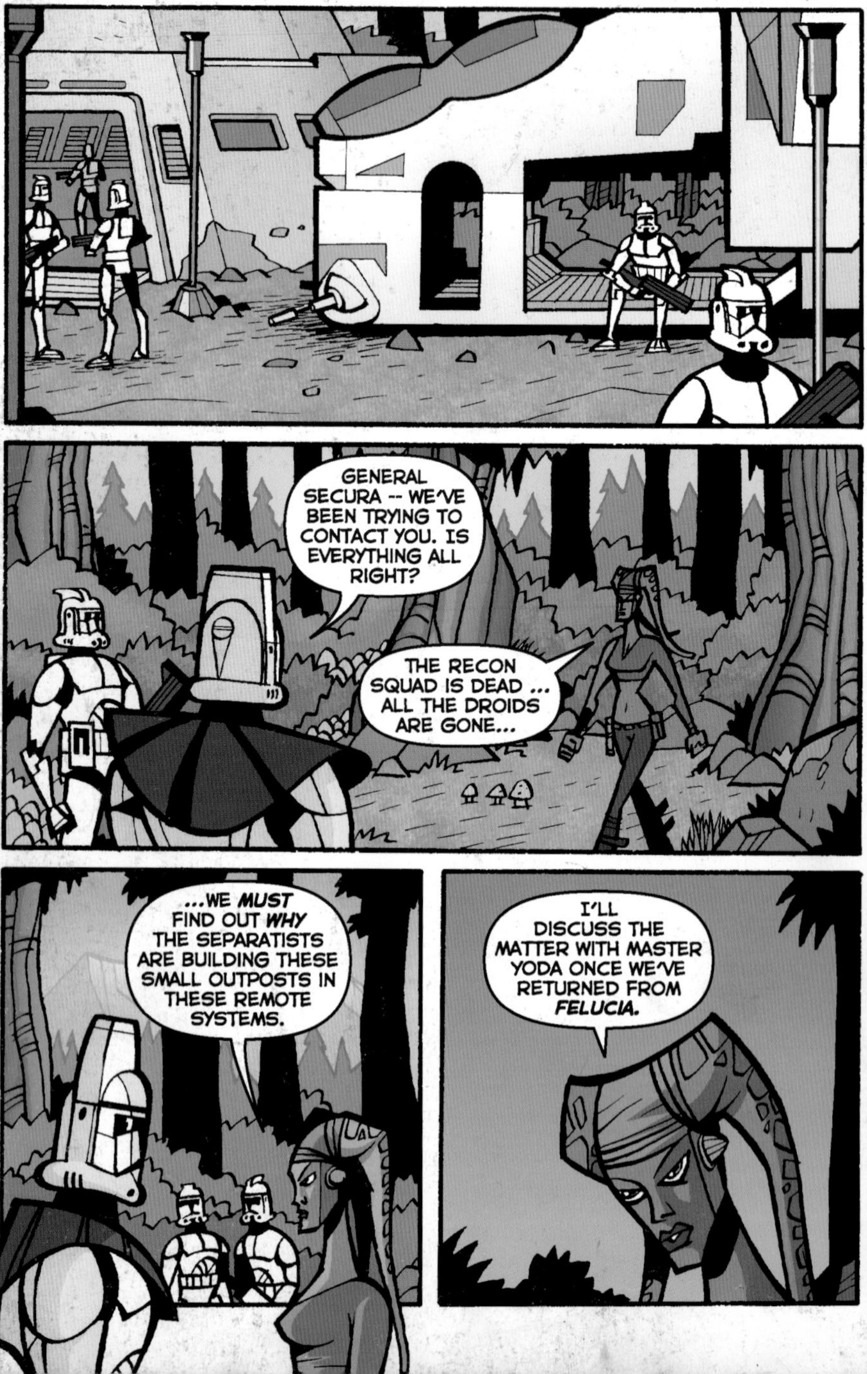
GENERAL SECURA -- WE'VE BEEN TRYING TO CONTACT YOU. IS EVERYTHING ALL RIGHT?
THE RECON SQUAD IS DEAD ... ALL THE DROIDS ARE GONE...
...WE *MUST* FIND OUT *WHY* THE SEPARATISTS ARE BUILDING THESE SMALL OUTPOSTS IN THESE REMOTE SYSTEMS.
I'LL DISCUSS THE MATTER WITH MASTER YODA ONCE WE'VE RETURNED FROM *FELUCIA.*

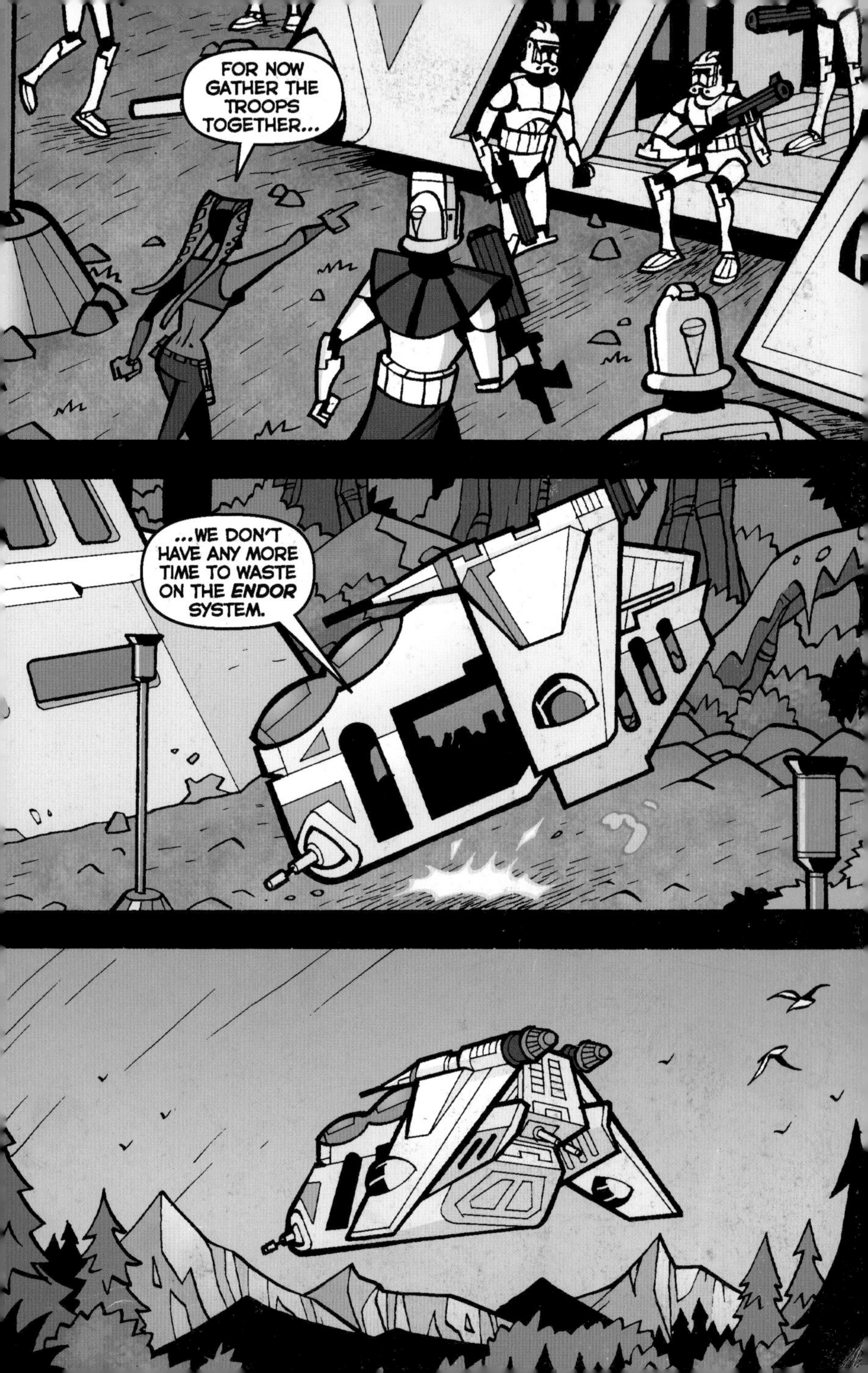
FOR NOW GATHER THE TROOPS TOGETHER...
...WE DON'T HAVE ANY MORE TIME TO WASTE ON THE *ENDOR* SYSTEM.

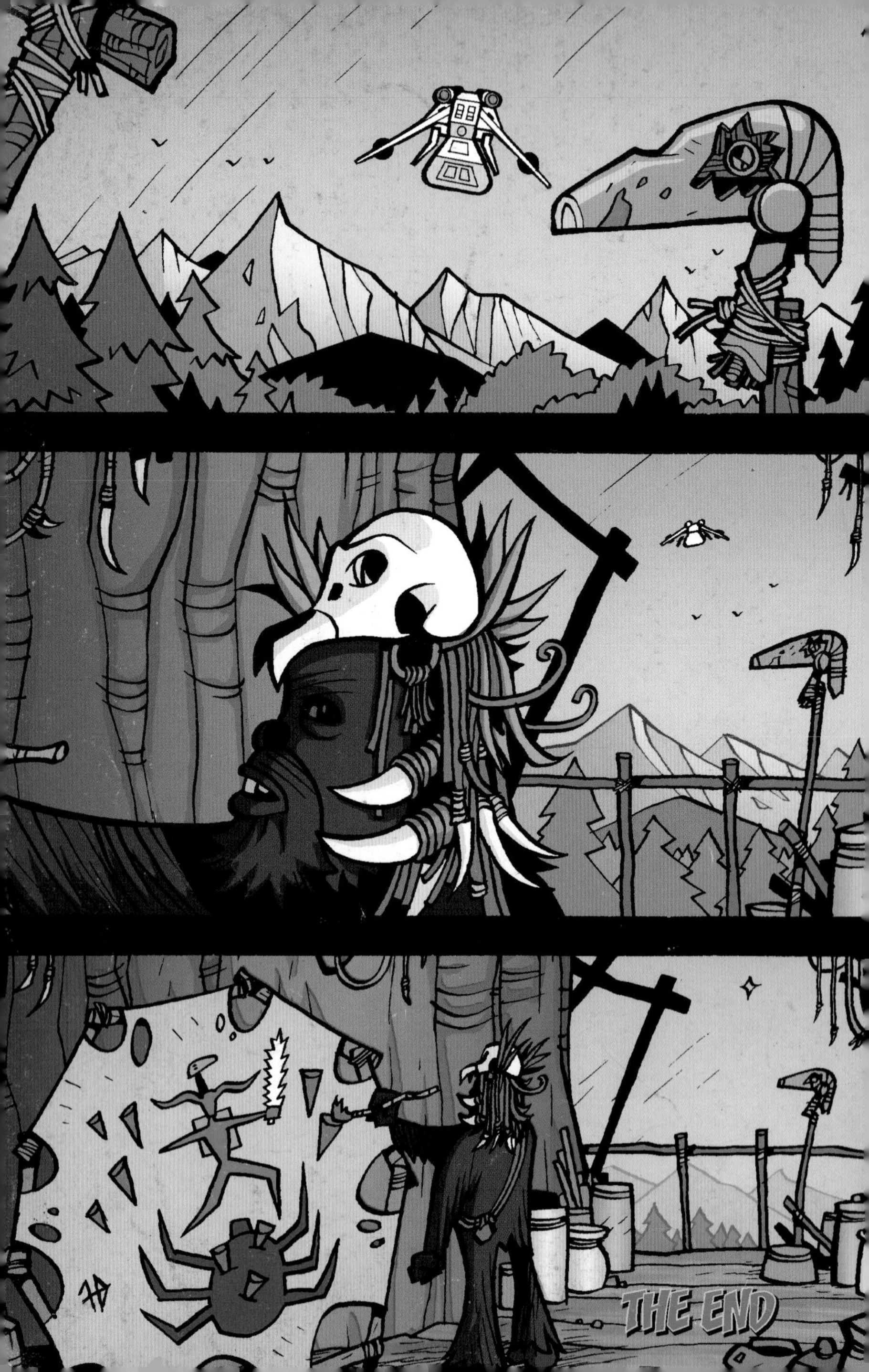
THE END

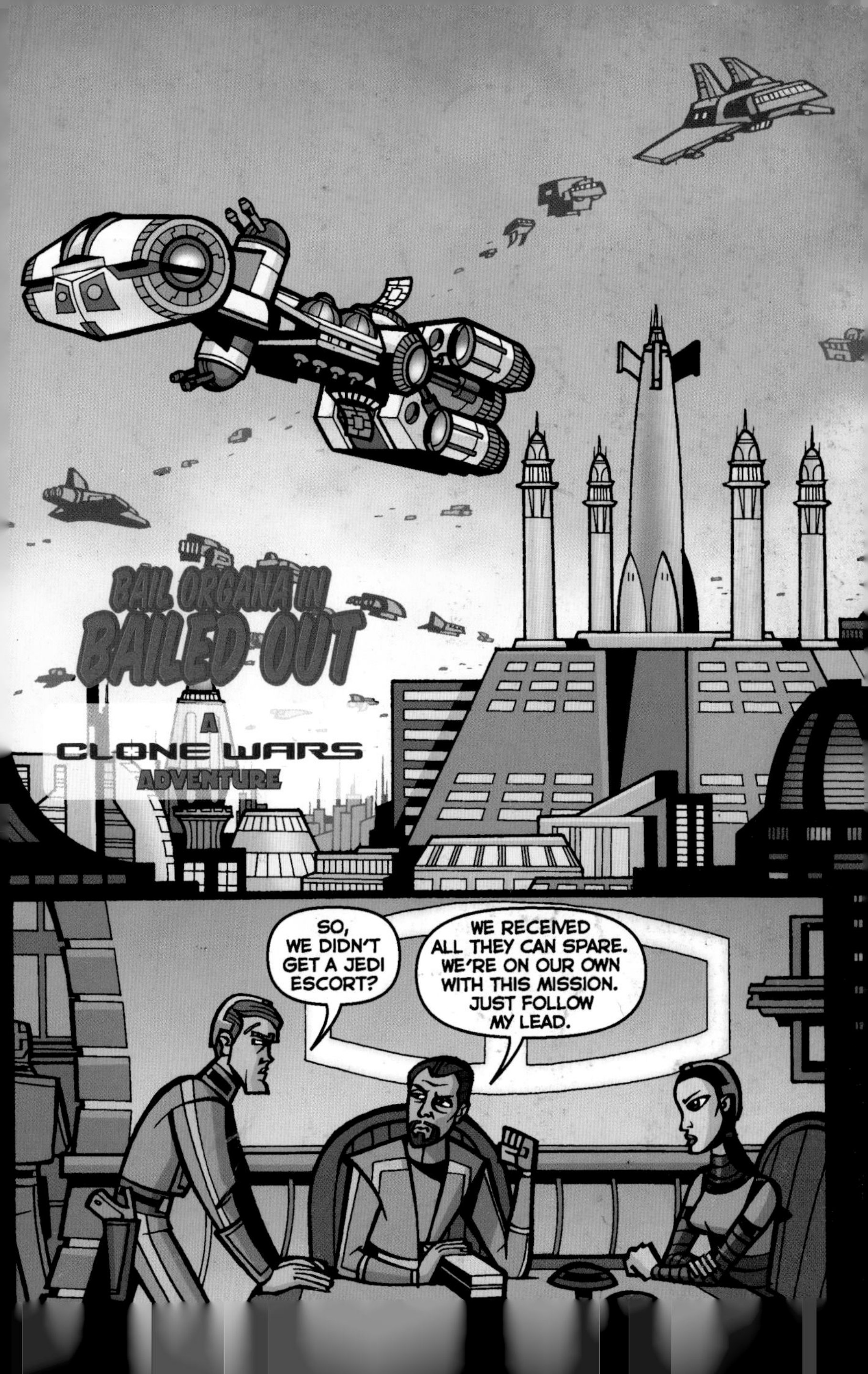
BAIL ORGANA IN
BAILED OUT
A CLONE WARS ADVENTURE
SO, WE DIDN'T GET A JEDI ESCORT?
WE RECEIVED ALL THEY CAN SPARE. WE'RE ON OUR OWN WITH THIS MISSION. JUST FOLLOW MY LEAD.

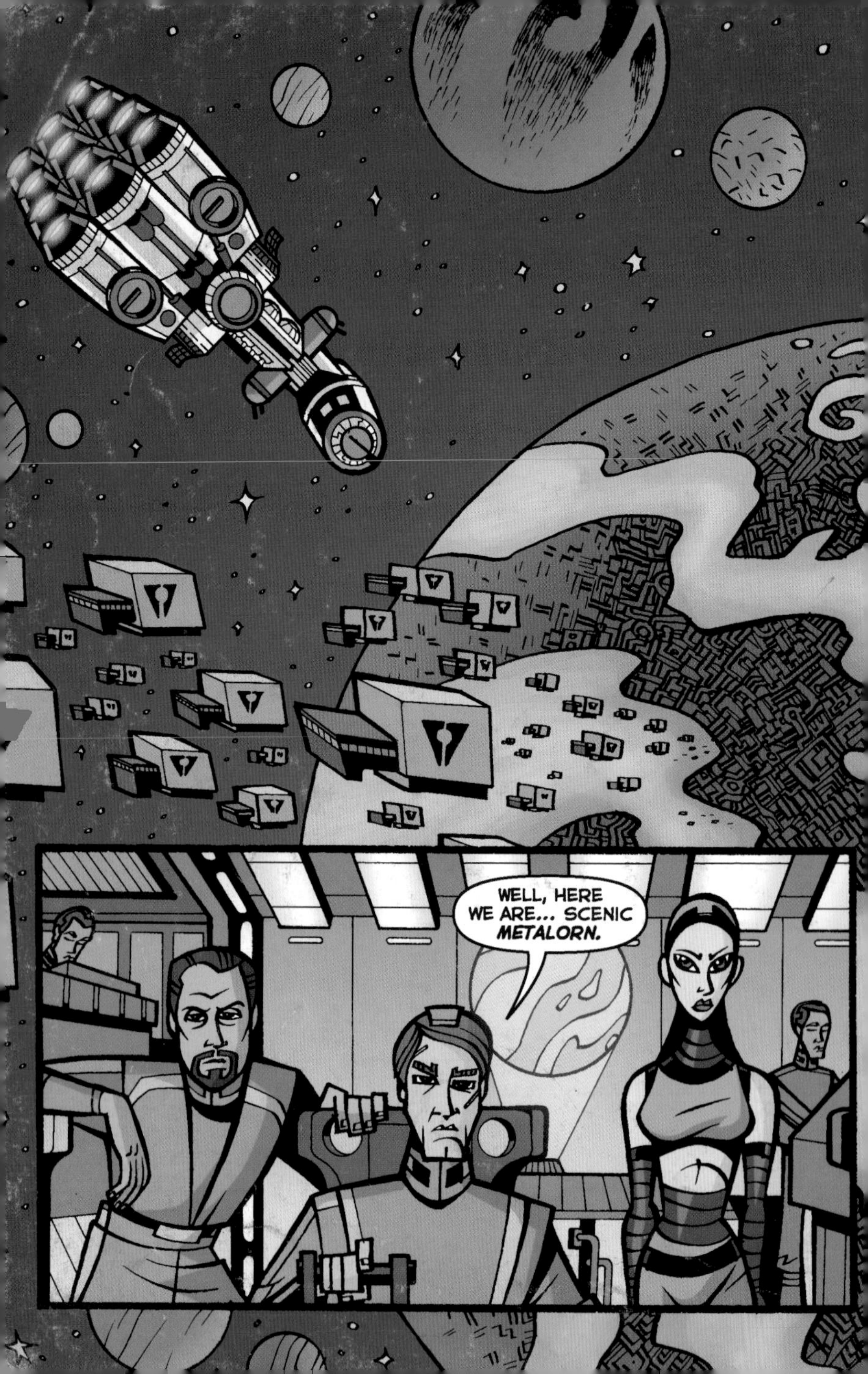
WELL, HERE WE ARE... SCENIC *METALORN.*

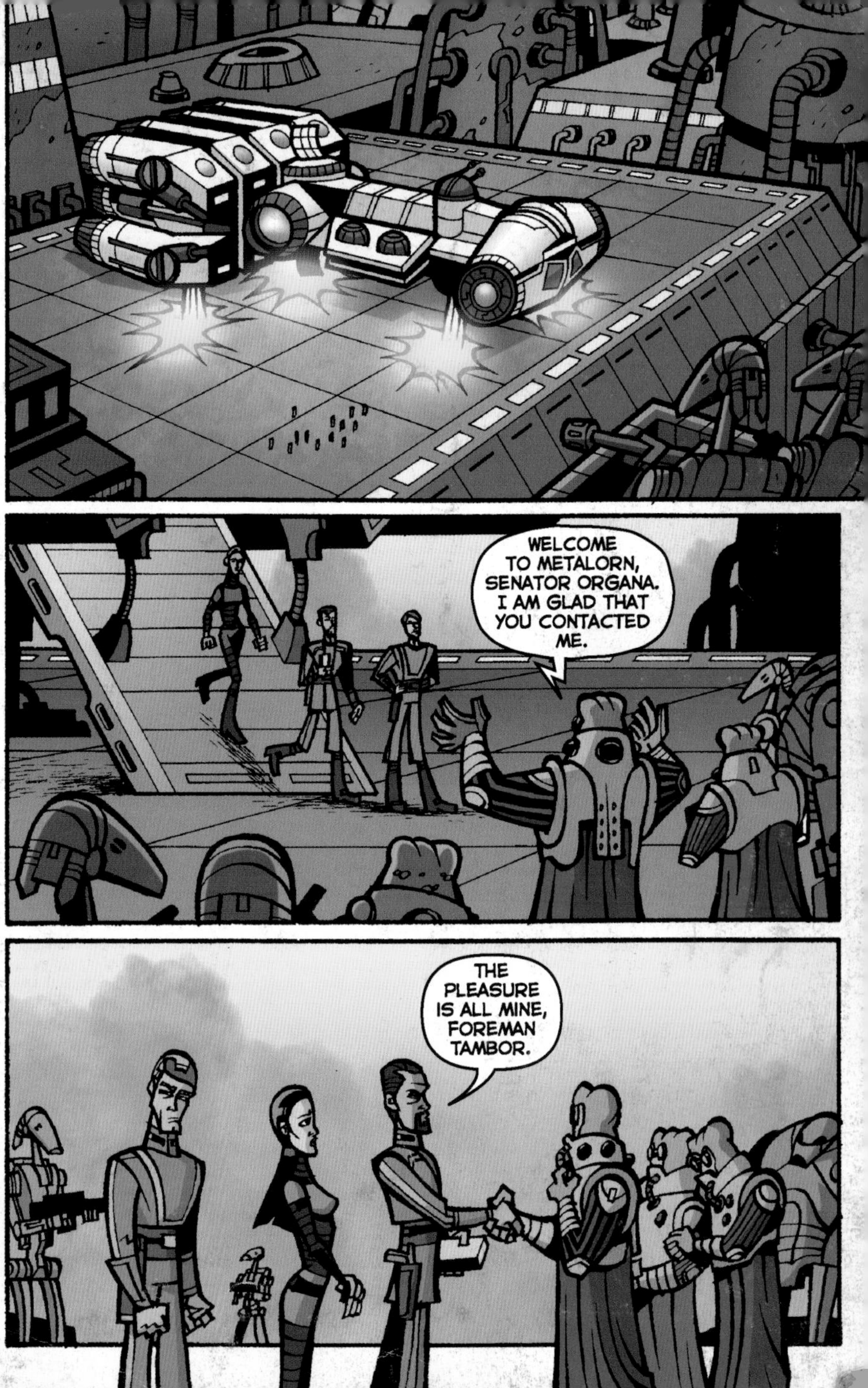
WELCOME TO METALORN, SENATOR ORGANA. I AM GLAD THAT YOU CONTACTED ME.
THE PLEASURE IS ALL MINE, FOREMAN TAMBOR.

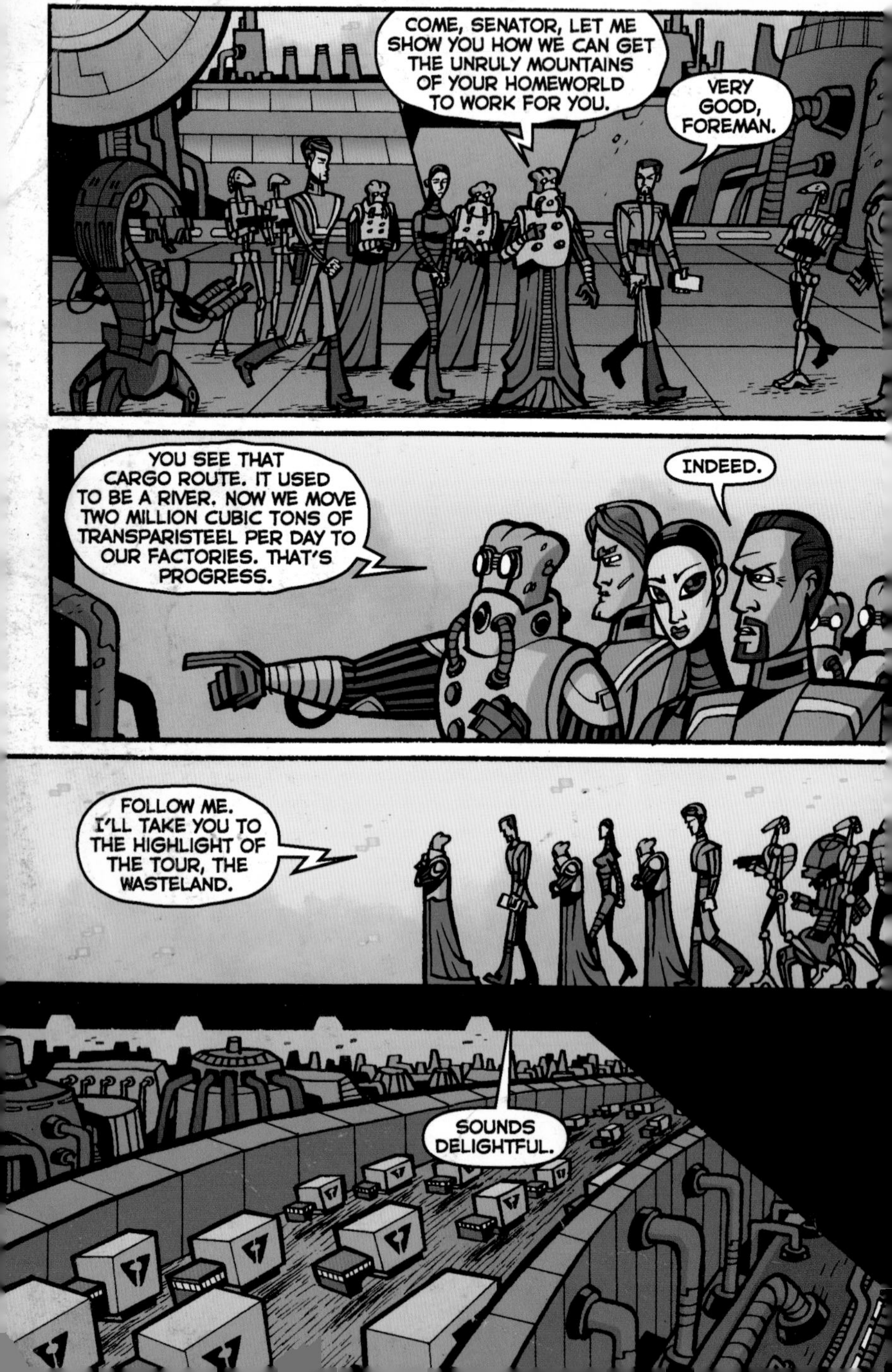
COME, SENATOR, LET ME SHOW YOU HOW WE CAN GET THE UNRULY MOUNTAINS OF YOUR HOMEWORLD TO WORK FOR YOU.
VERY GOOD, FOREMAN.
YOU SEE THAT CARGO ROUTE. IT USED TO BE A RIVER. NOW WE MOVE TWO MILLION CUBIC TONS OF TRANSPARISTEEL PER DAY TO OUR FACTORIES. THAT'S PROGRESS.
INDEED.
FOLLOW ME. I'LL TAKE YOU TO THE HIGHLIGHT OF THE TOUR, THE WASTELAND.
SOUNDS DELIGHTFUL.

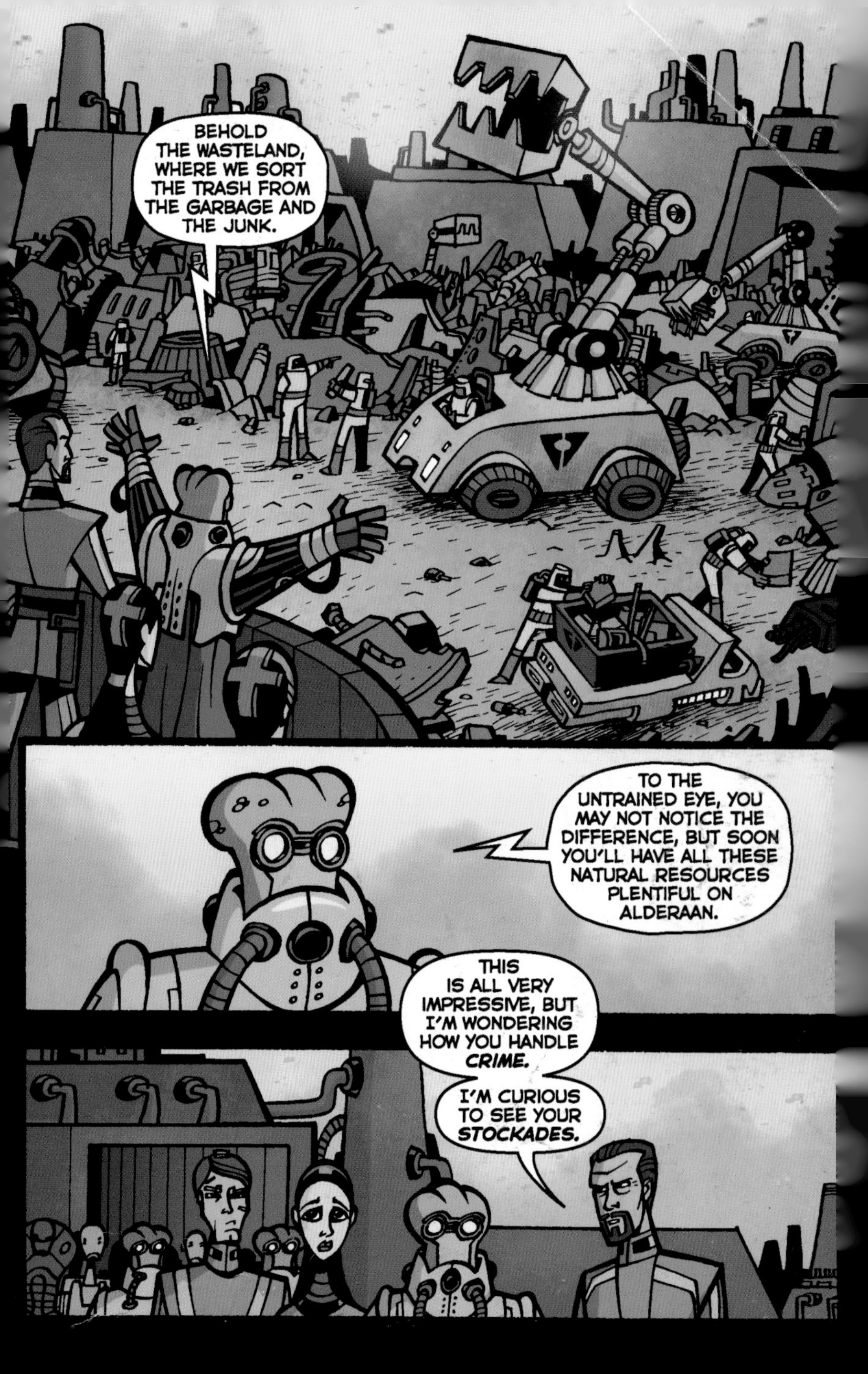
BEHOLD THE WASTELAND, WHERE WE SORT THE TRASH FROM THE GARBAGE AND THE JUNK.
TO THE UNTRAINED EYE, YOU MAY NOT NOTICE THE DIFFERENCE, BUT SOON YOU'LL HAVE ALL THESE NATURAL RESOURCES PLENTIFUL ON ALDERAAN.
THIS IS ALL VERY IMPRESSIVE, BUT I'M WONDERING HOW YOU HANDLE *CRIME.*
I'M CURIOUS TO SEE YOUR *STOCKADES.*

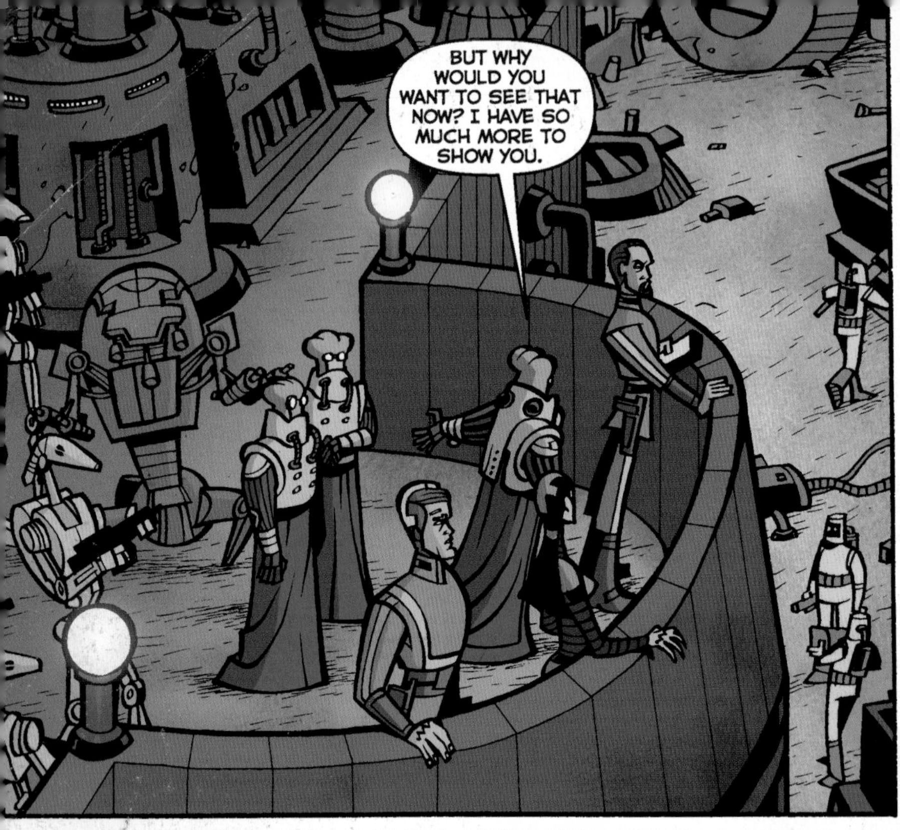
BUT WHY WOULD YOU WANT TO SEE THAT NOW? I HAVE SO MUCH MORE TO SHOW YOU.

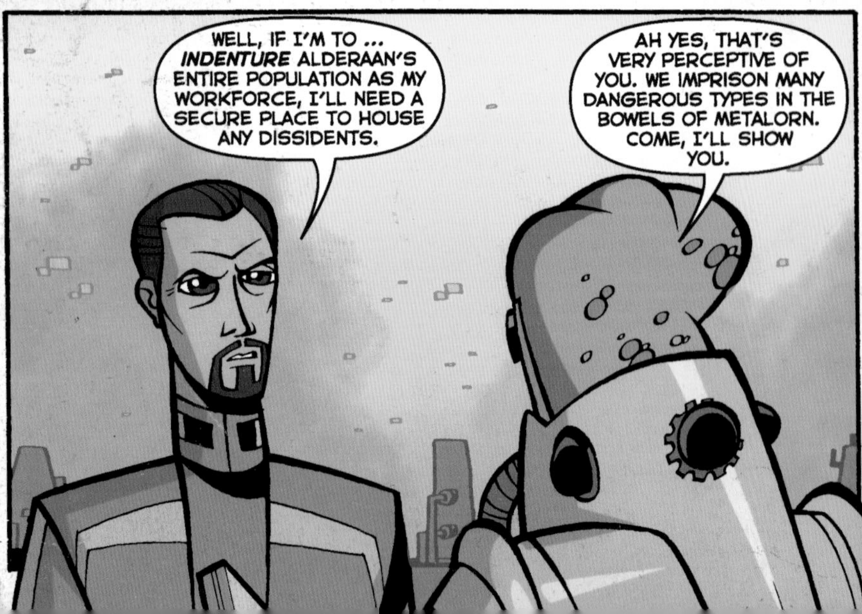
WELL, IF I'M TO ... *INDENTURE* ALDERAAN'S ENTIRE POPULATION AS MY WORKFORCE, I'LL NEED A SECURE PLACE TO HOUSE ANY DISSIDENTS.
AH YES, THAT'S VERY PERCEPTIVE OF YOU. WE IMPRISON MANY DANGEROUS TYPES IN THE BOWELS OF METALORN. COME, I'LL SHOW YOU.

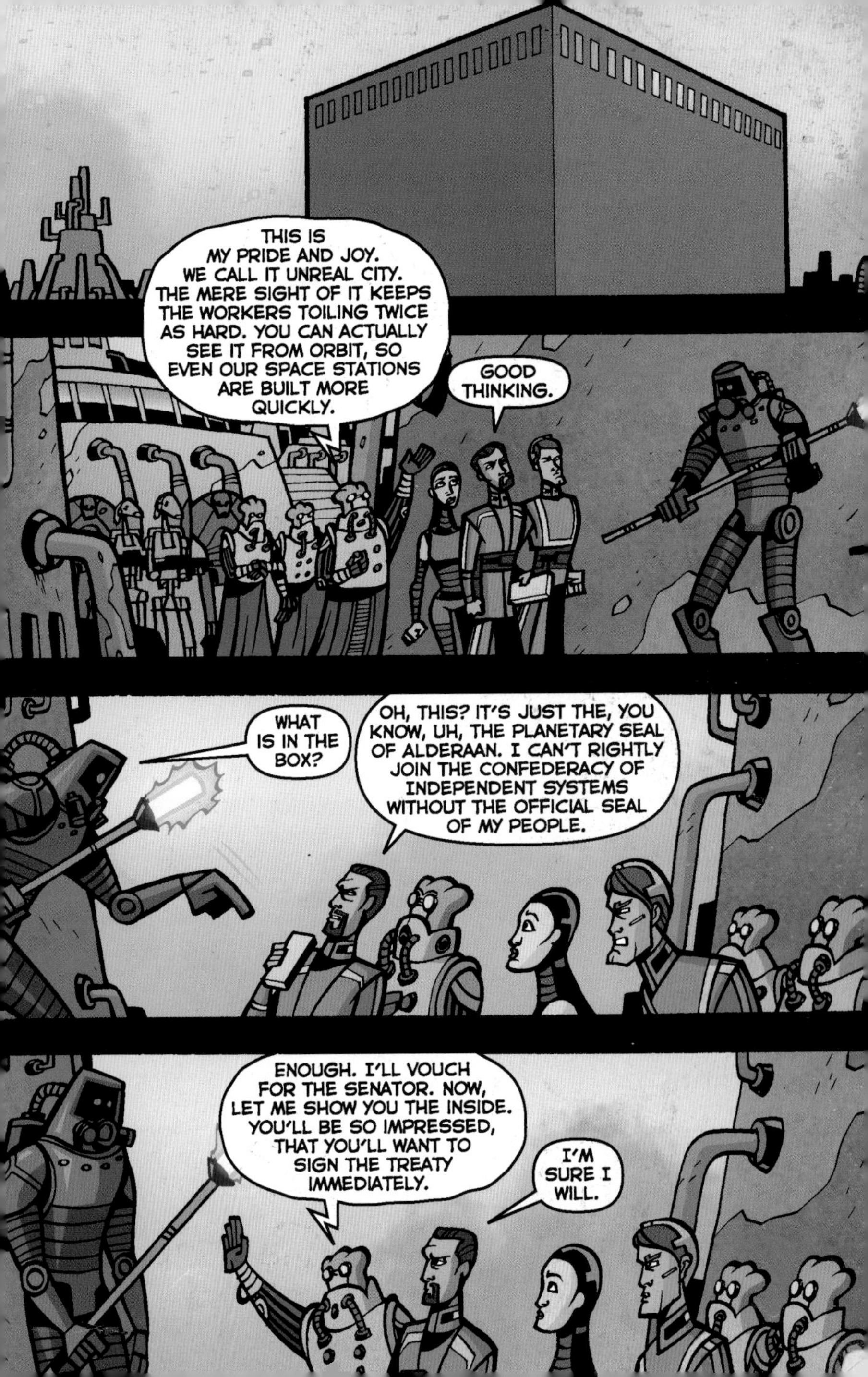
THIS IS MY PRIDE AND JOY. WE CALL IT UNREAL CITY. THE MERE SIGHT OF IT KEEPS THE WORKERS TOILING TWICE AS HARD. YOU CAN ACTUALLY SEE IT FROM ORBIT, SO EVEN OUR SPACE STATIONS ARE BUILT MORE QUICKLY.
GOOD THINKING.
WHAT IS IN THE BOX?
OH, THIS? IT'S JUST THE, YOU KNOW, UH, THE PLANETARY SEAL OF ALDERAAN. I CAN'T RIGHTLY JOIN THE CONFEDERACY OF INDEPENDENT SYSTEMS WITHOUT THE OFFICIAL SEAL OF MY PEOPLE.
ENOUGH. I'LL VOUCH FOR THE SENATOR. NOW, LET ME SHOW YOU THE INSIDE. YOU'LL BE SO IMPRESSED, THAT YOU'LL WANT TO SIGN THE TREATY IMMEDIATELY.
I'M SURE I WILL.

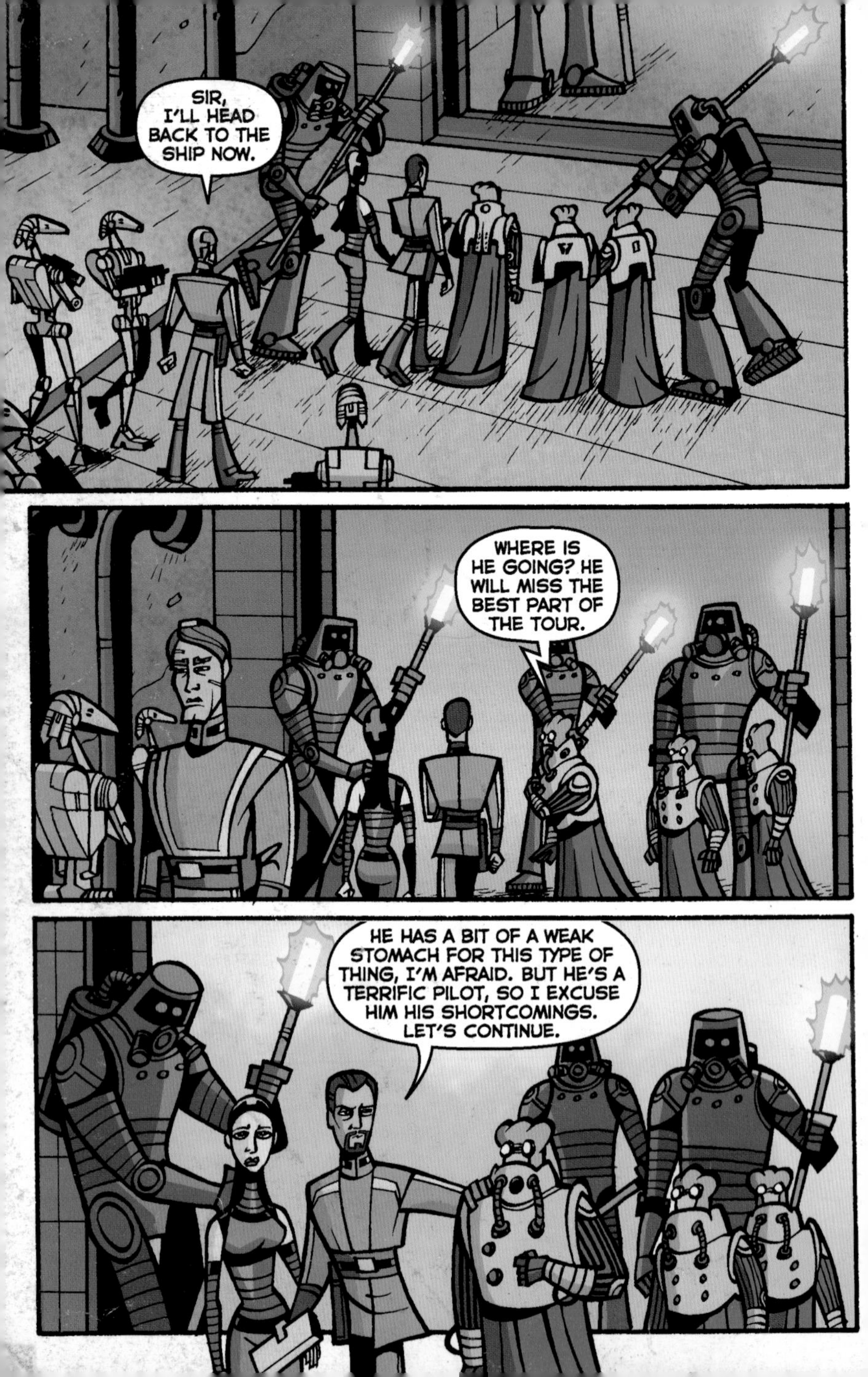
SIR, I'LL HEAD BACK TO THE SHIP NOW.
WHERE IS HE GOING? HE WILL MISS THE BEST PART OF THE TOUR.
HE HAS A BIT OF A WEAK STOMACH FOR THIS TYPE OF THING, I'M AFRAID. BUT HE'S A TERRIFIC PILOT, SO I EXCUSE HIM HIS SHORTCOMINGS. LET'S CONTINUE.

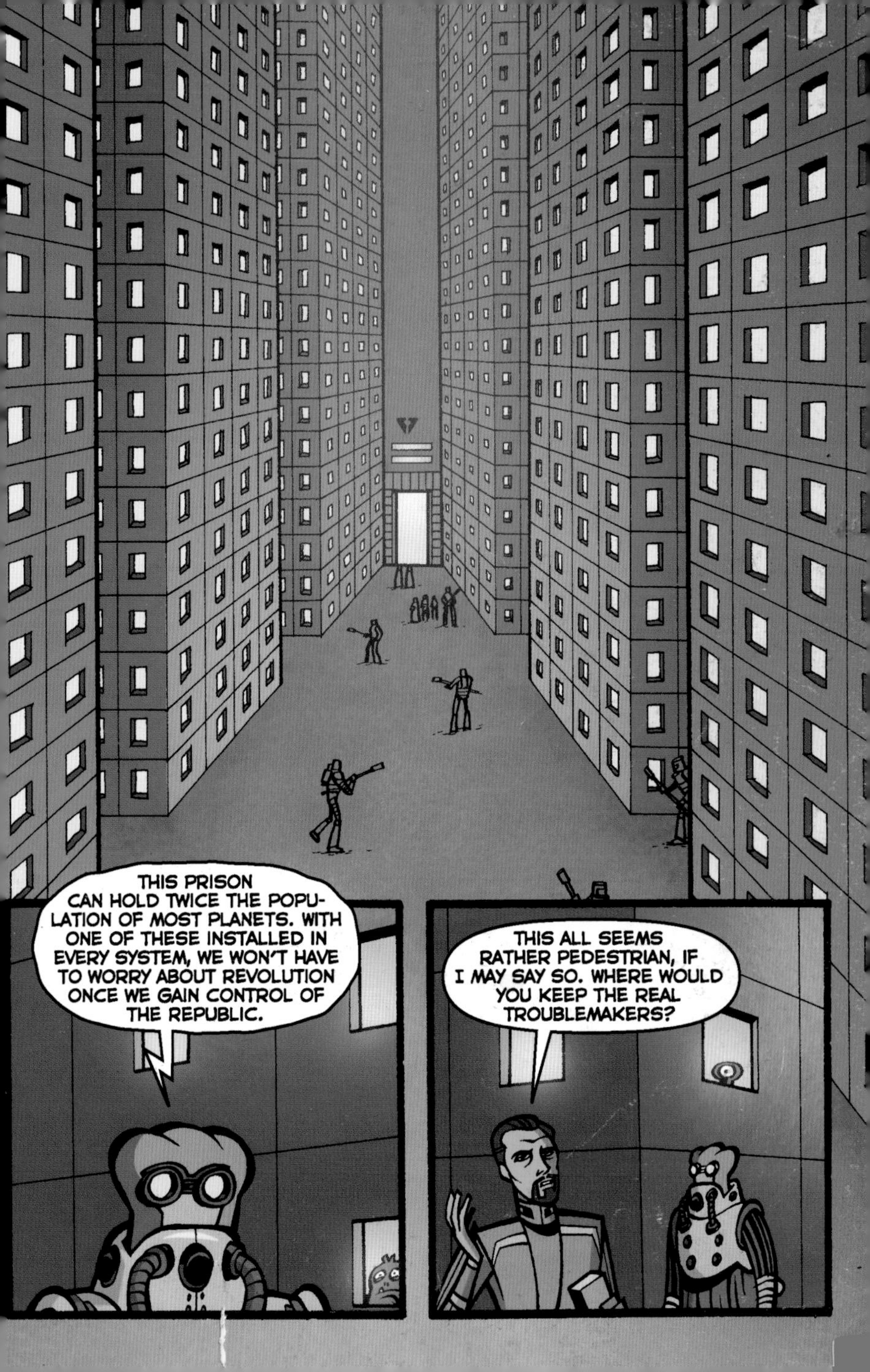
THIS PRISON CAN HOLD TWICE THE POPULATION OF MOST PLANETS. WITH ONE OF THESE INSTALLED IN EVERY SYSTEM, WE WON'T HAVE TO WORRY ABOUT REVOLUTION ONCE WE GAIN CONTROL OF THE REPUBLIC.
THIS ALL SEEMS RATHER PEDESTRIAN, IF I MAY SAY SO. WHERE WOULD YOU KEEP THE REAL TROUBLEMAKERS?

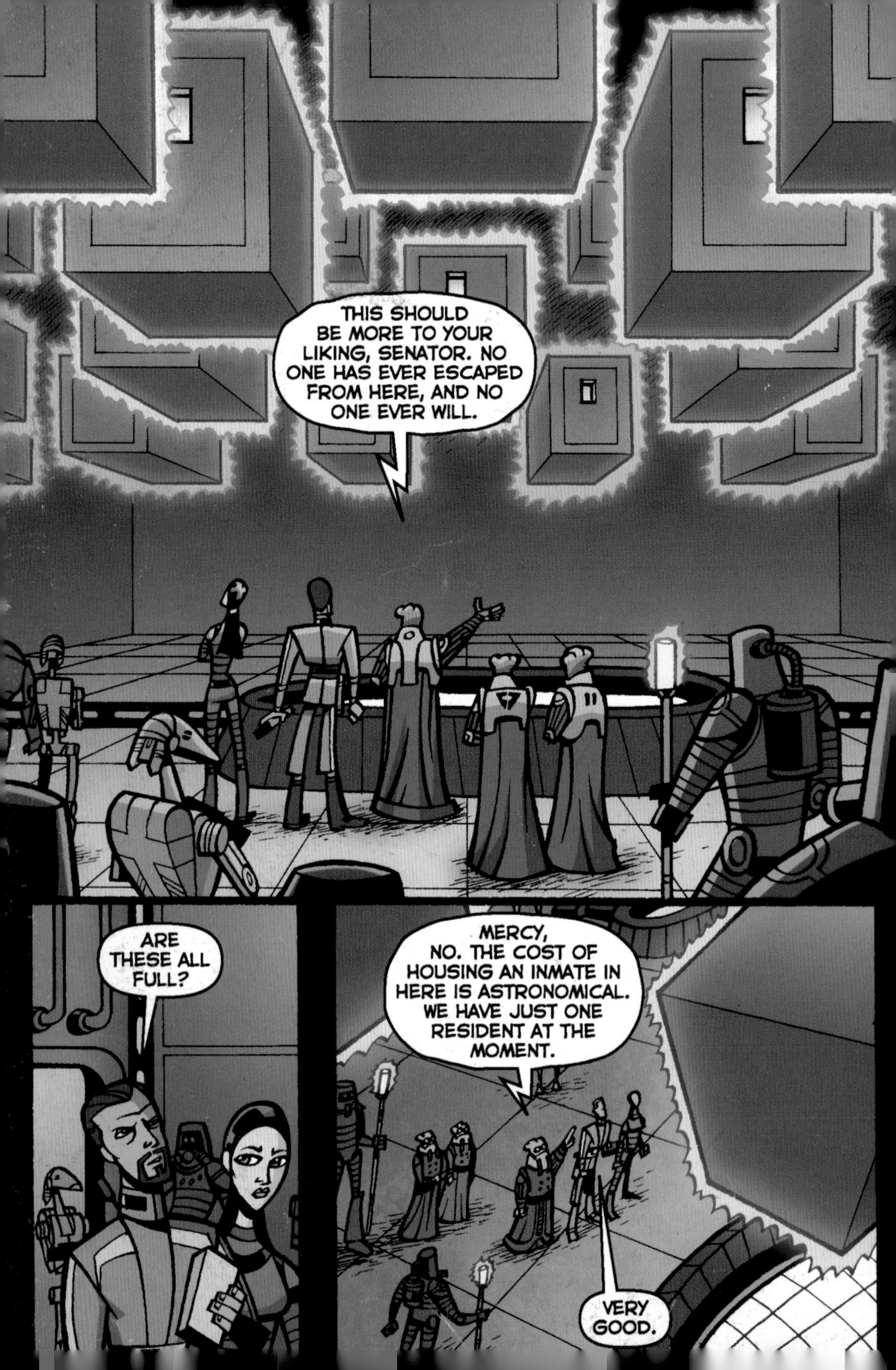
THIS SHOULD BE MORE TO YOUR LIKING, SENATOR. NO ONE HAS EVER ESCAPED FROM HERE, AND NO ONE EVER WILL.
ARE THESE ALL FULL?
MERCY, NO. THE COST OF HOUSING AN INMATE IN HERE IS ASTRONOMICAL. WE HAVE JUST ONE RESIDENT AT THE MOMENT.
VERY GOOD.

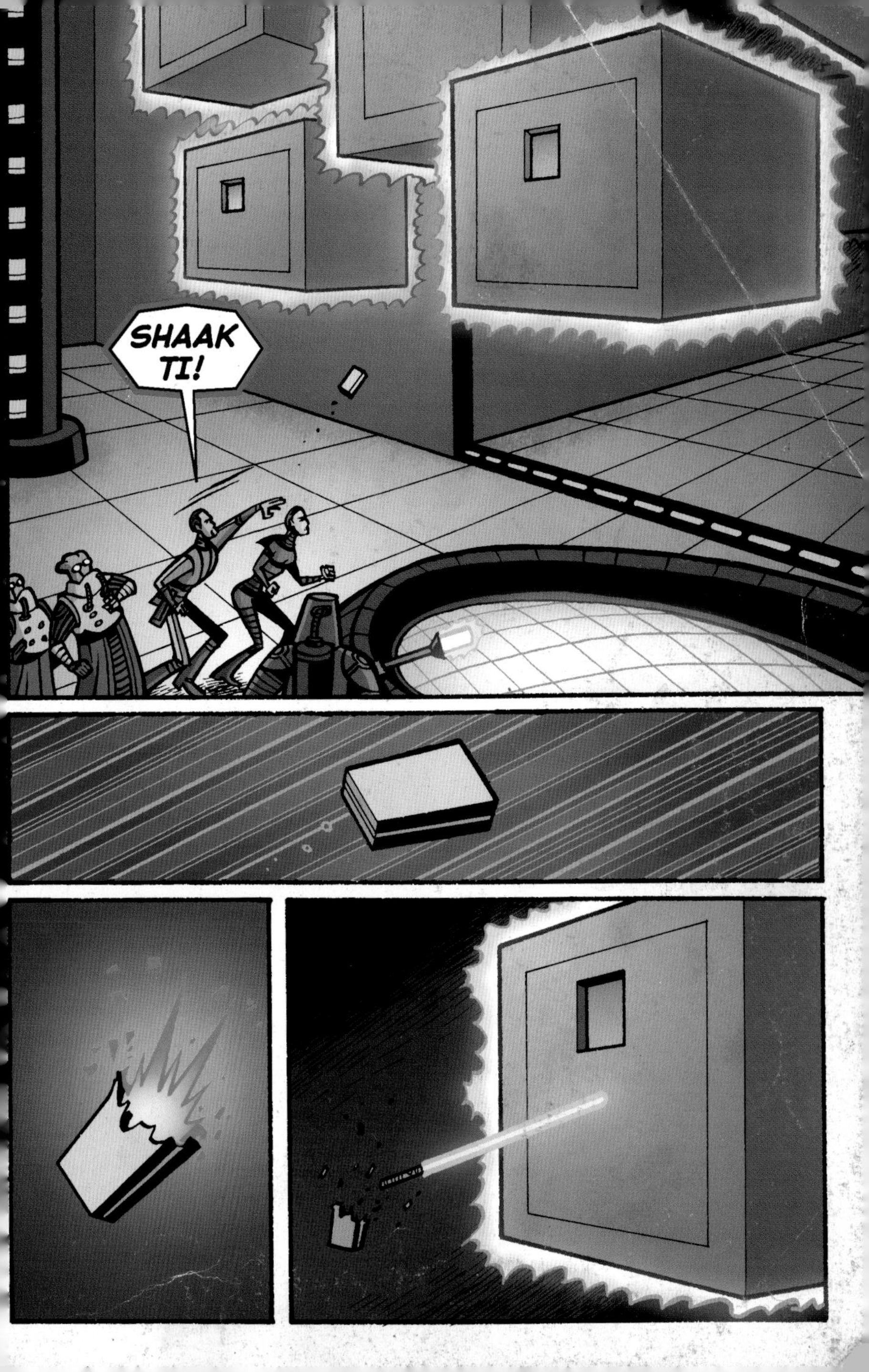
SHAAK TI!

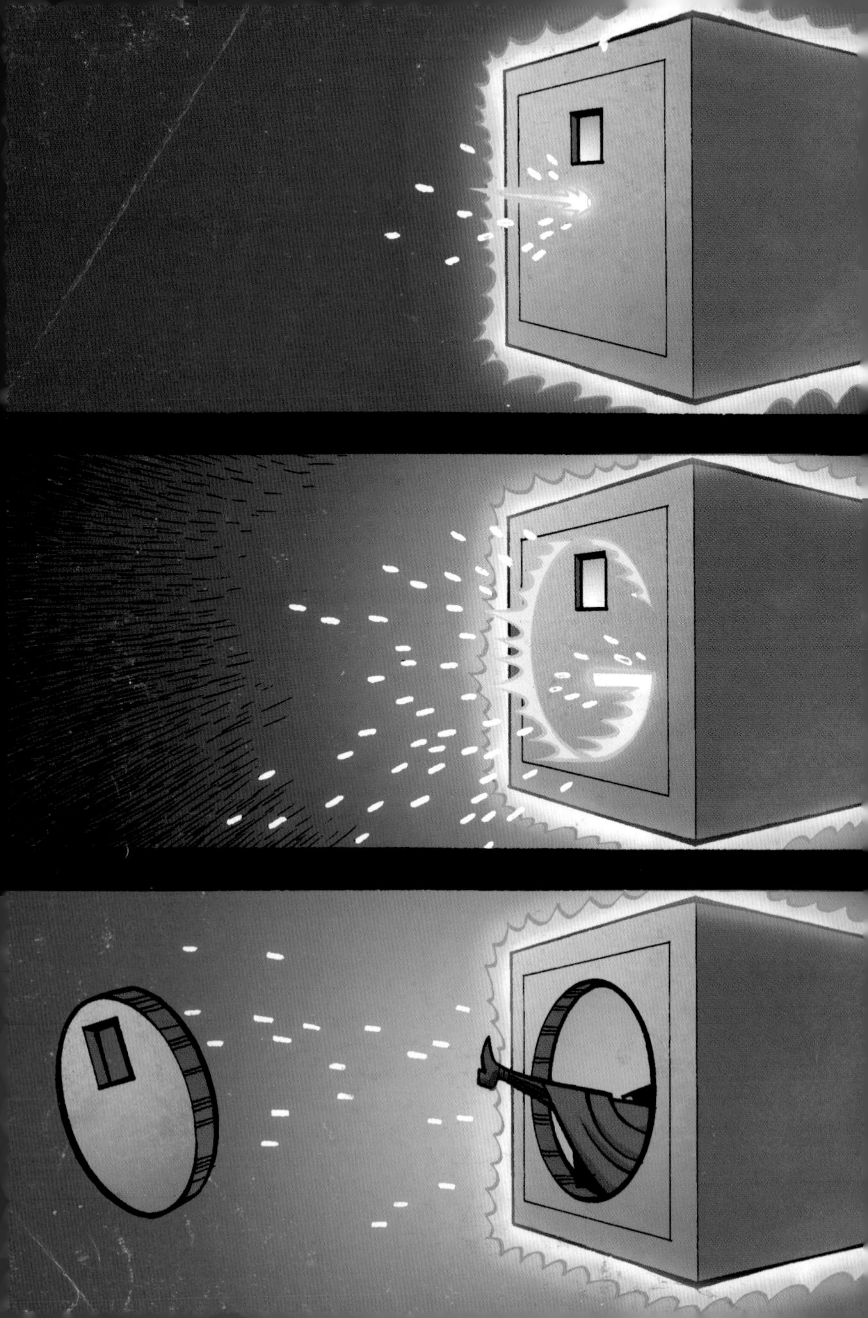

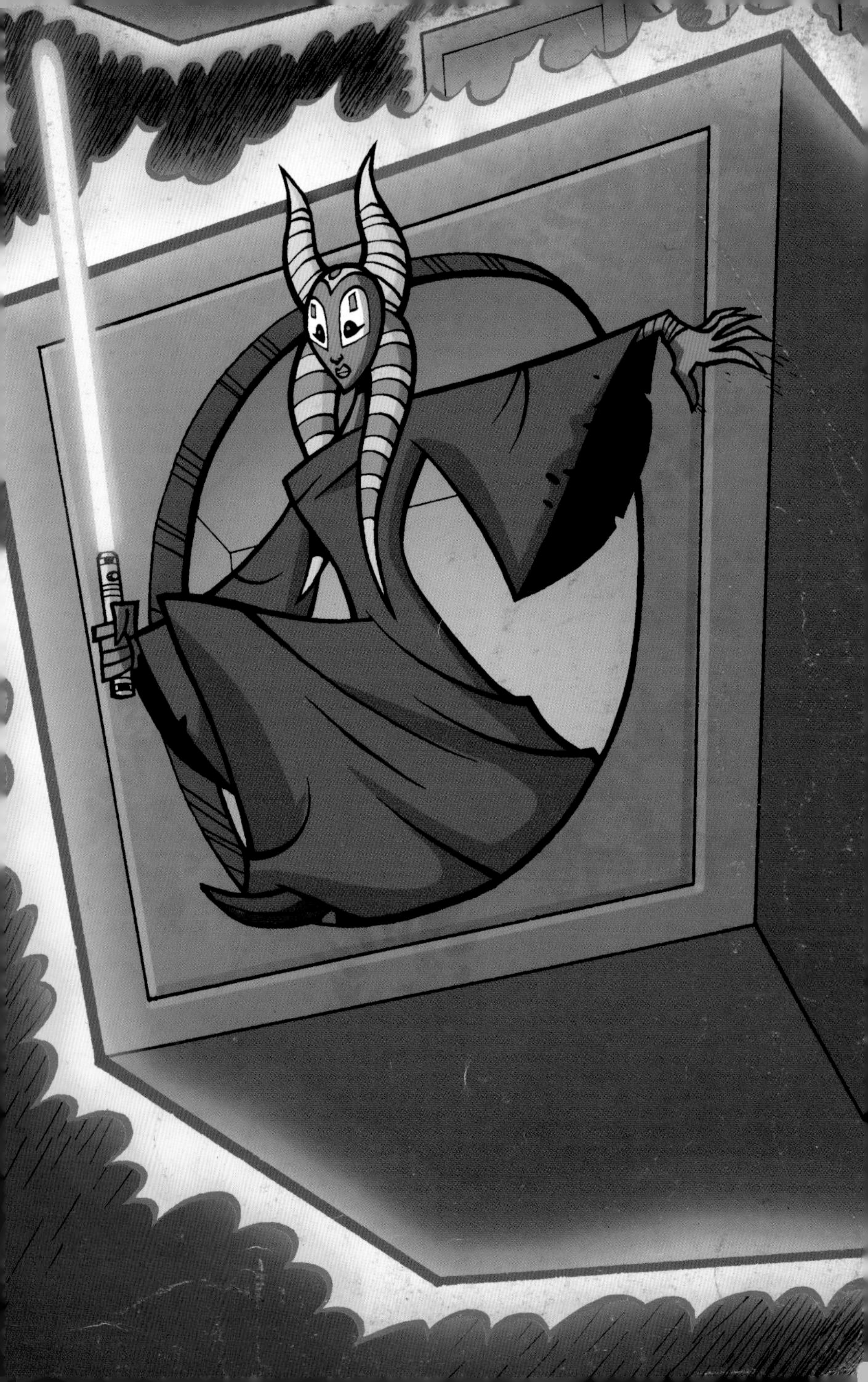

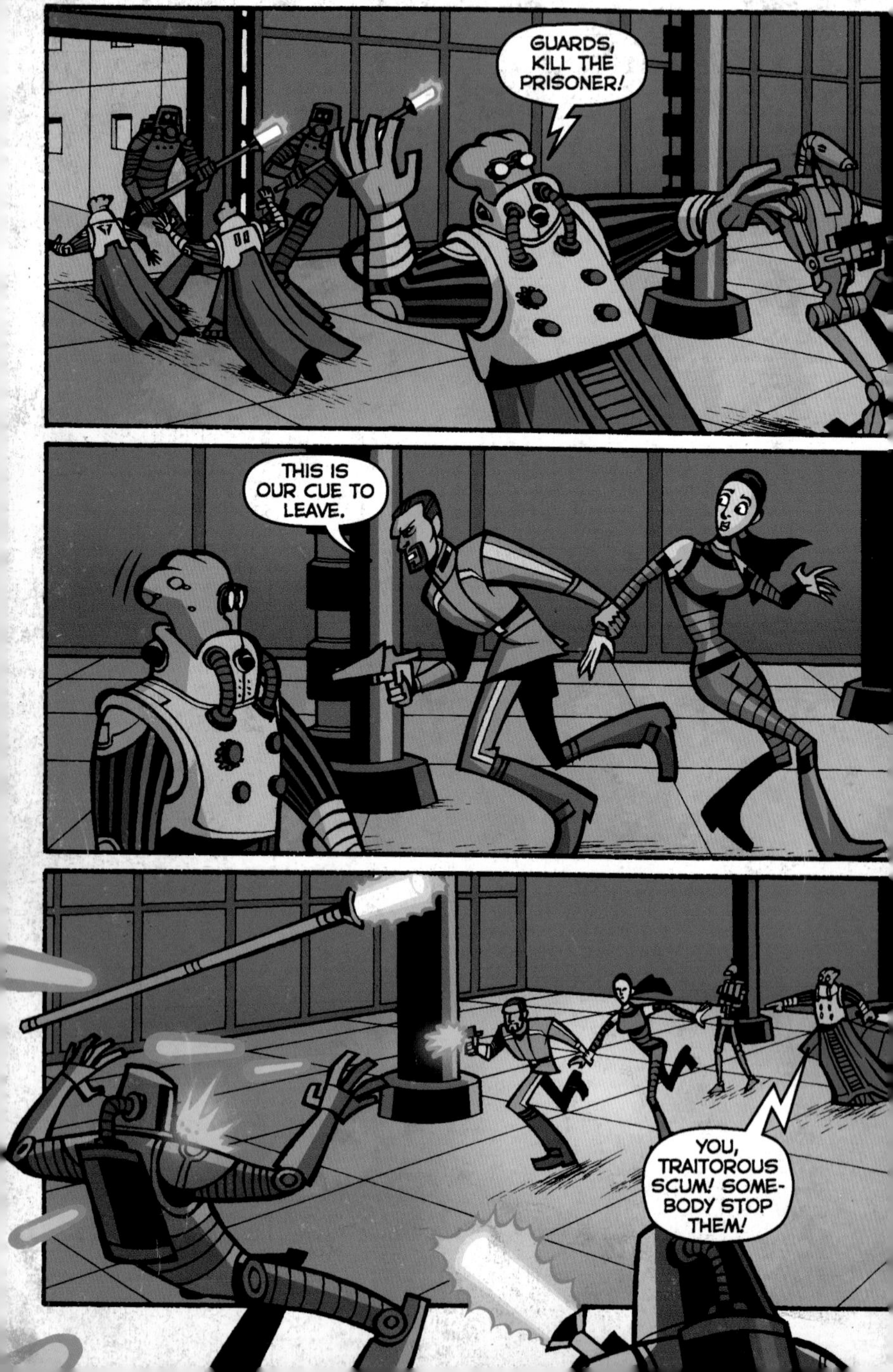
GUARDS, KILL THE PRISONER!
THIS IS OUR CUE TO LEAVE.
YOU, TRAITOROUS SCUM! SOME-BODY STOP THEM!

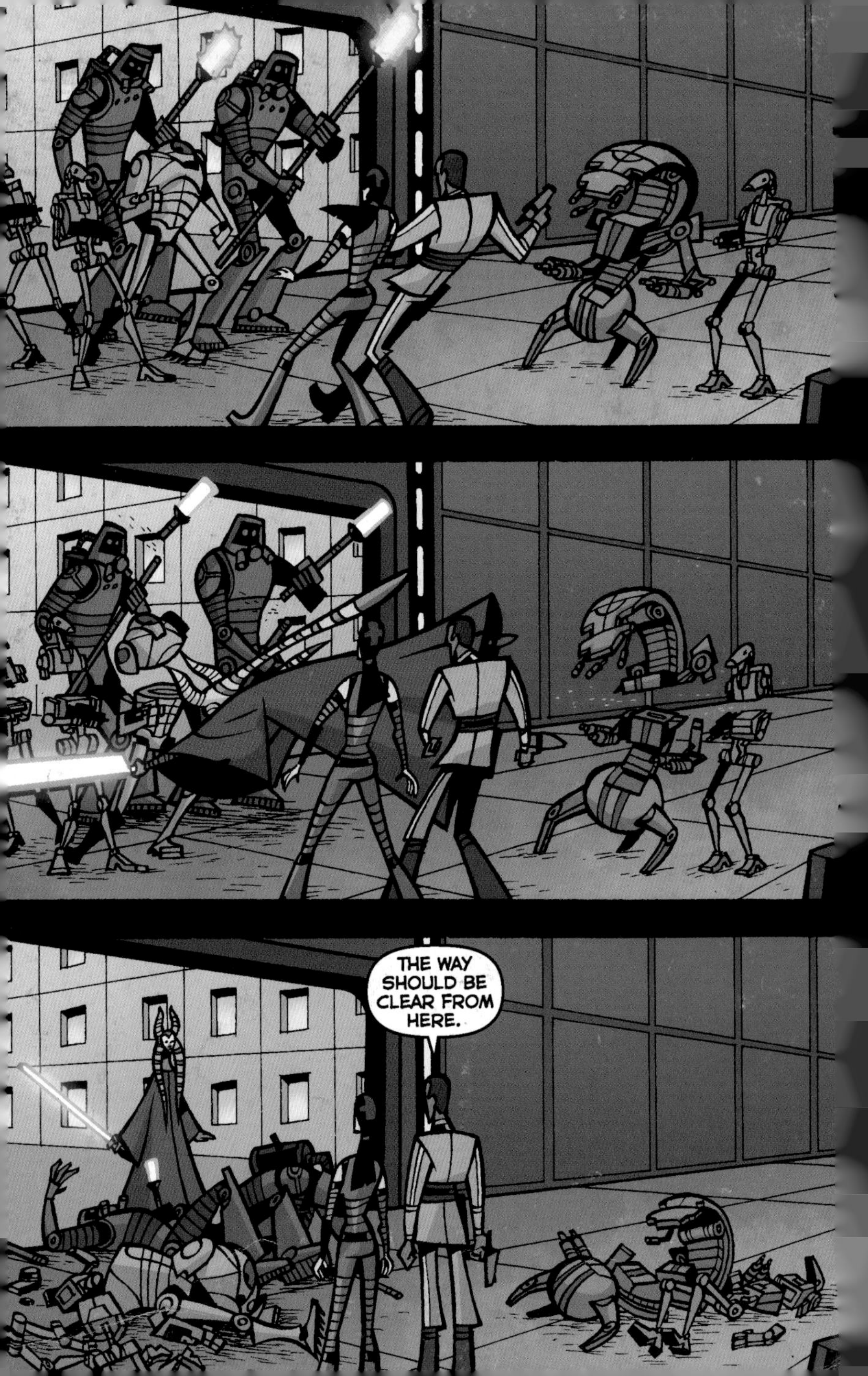
THE WAY SHOULD BE CLEAR FROM HERE.

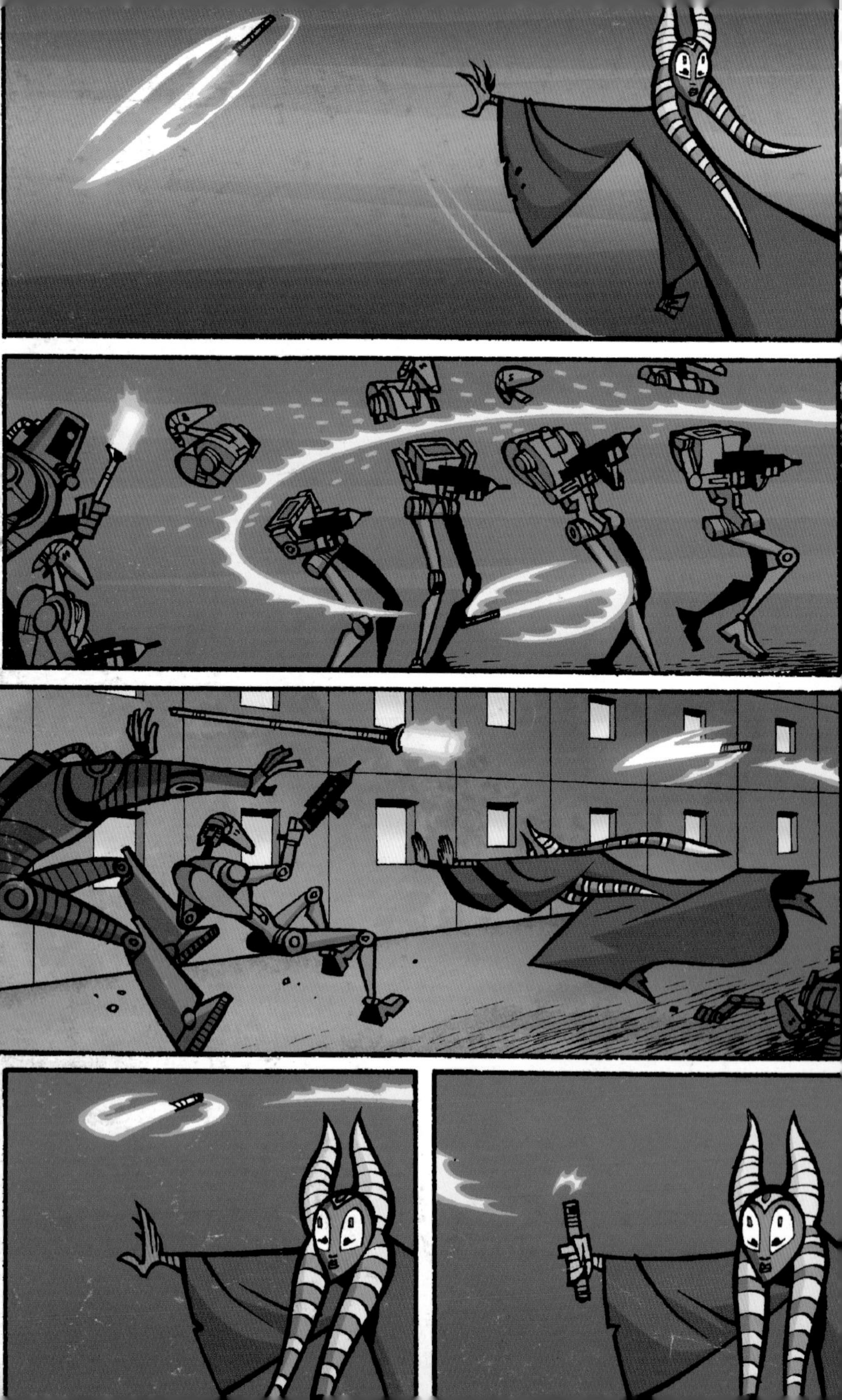

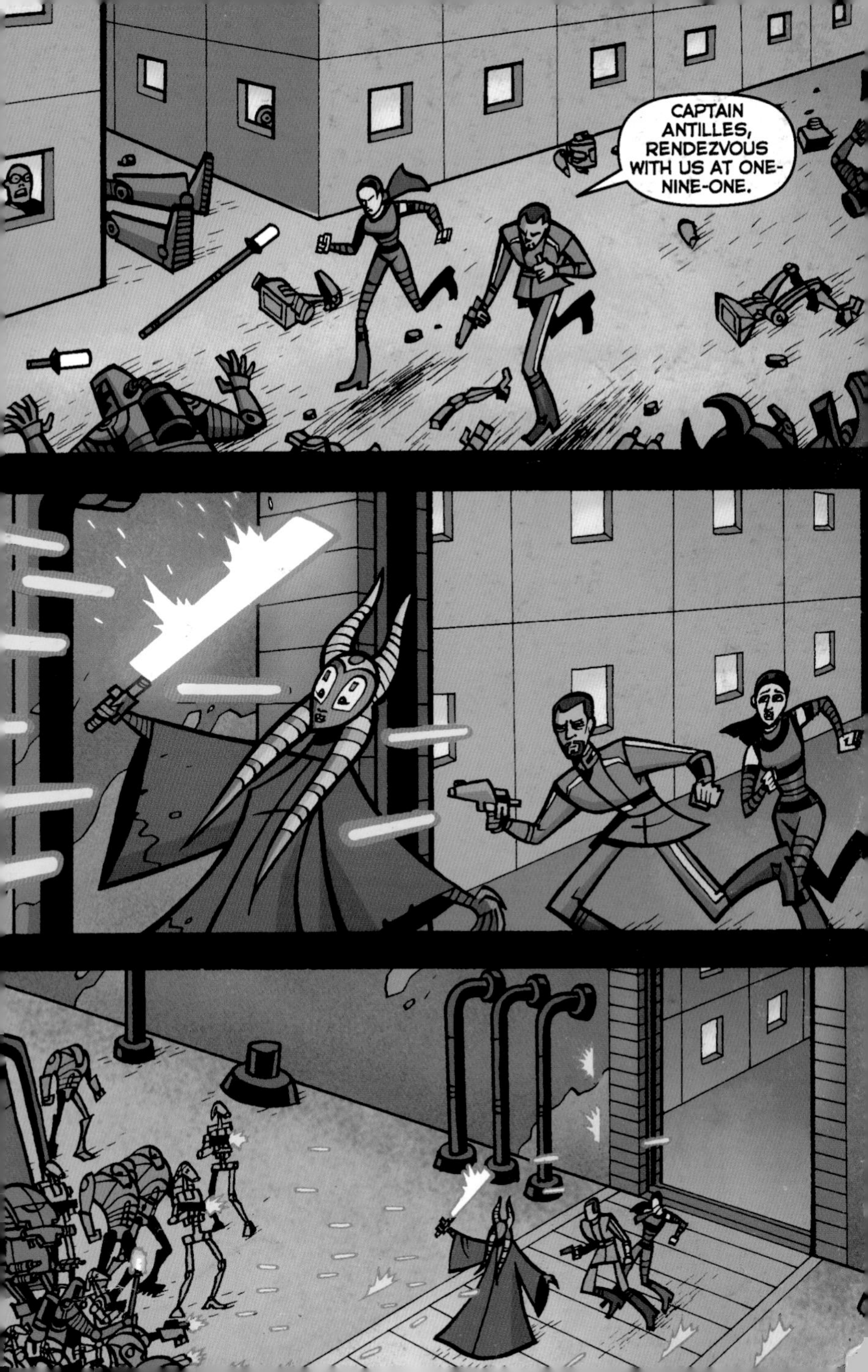
CAPTAIN ANTILLES, RENDEZVOUS WITH US AT ONE-NINE-ONE.

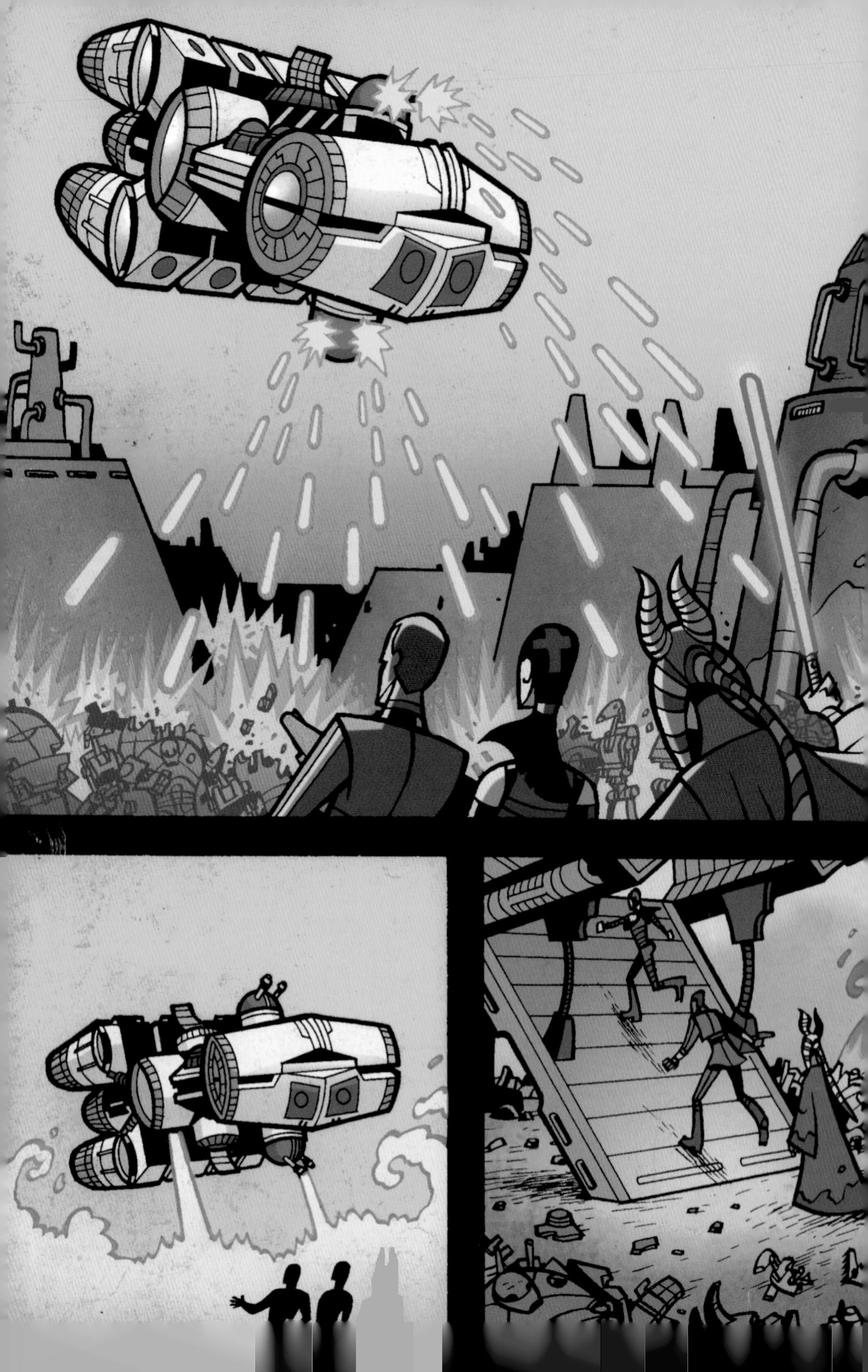

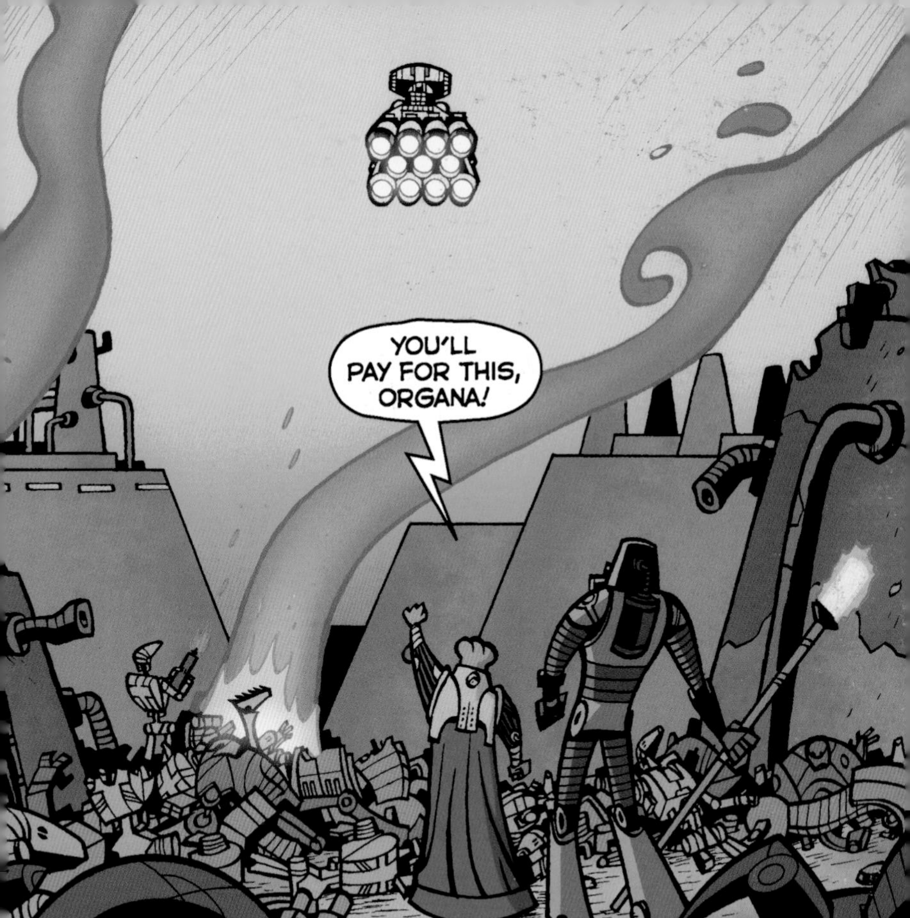
YOU'LL PAY FOR THIS, ORGANA!
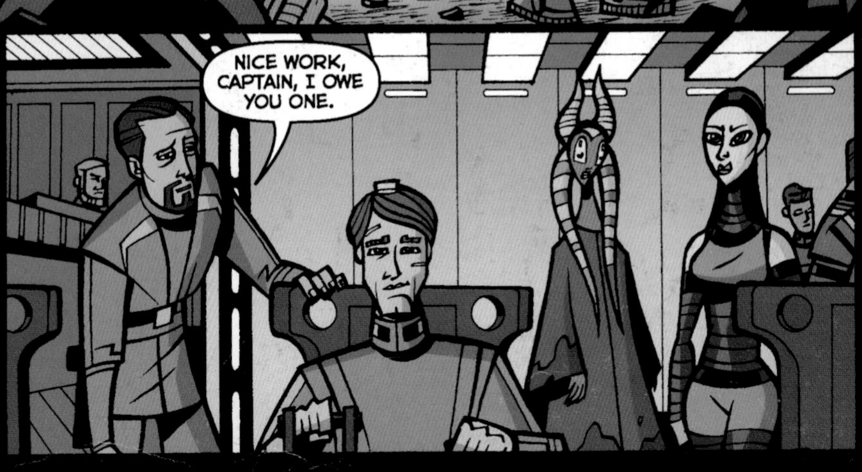
NICE WORK, CAPTAIN, I OWE YOU ONE.

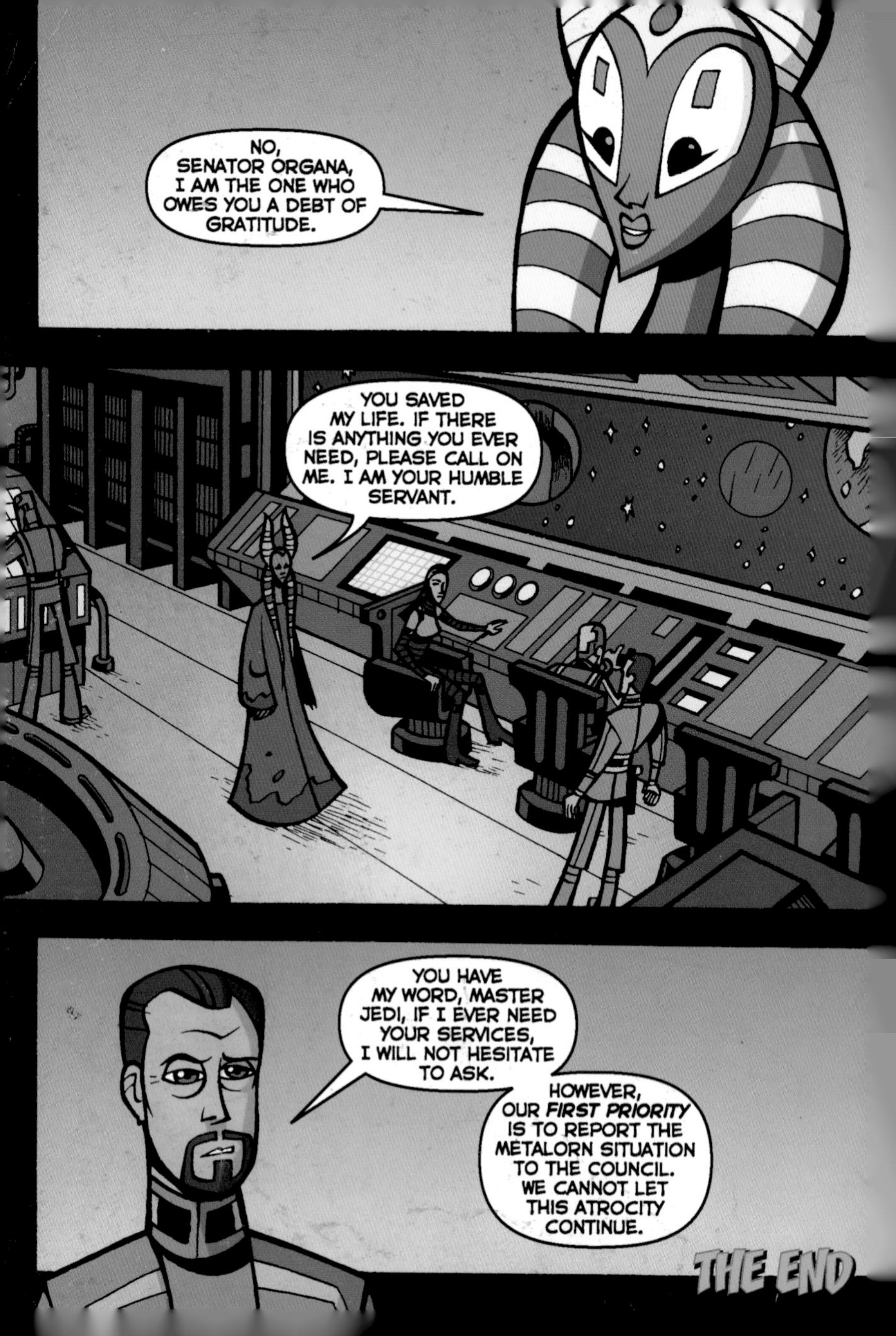
NO, SENATOR ORGANA, I AM THE ONE WHO OWES YOU A DEBT OF GRATITUDE.
YOU SAVED MY LIFE. IF THERE IS ANYTHING YOU EVER NEED, PLEASE CALL ON ME. I AM YOUR HUMBLE SERVANT.
YOU HAVE MY WORD, MASTER JEDI, IF I EVER NEED YOUR SERVICES, I WILL NOT HESITATE TO ASK.
HOWEVER, OUR FIRST PRIORITY IS TO REPORT THE METALORN SITUATION TO THE COUNCIL. WE CANNOT LET THIS ATROCITY CONTINUE.
THE END

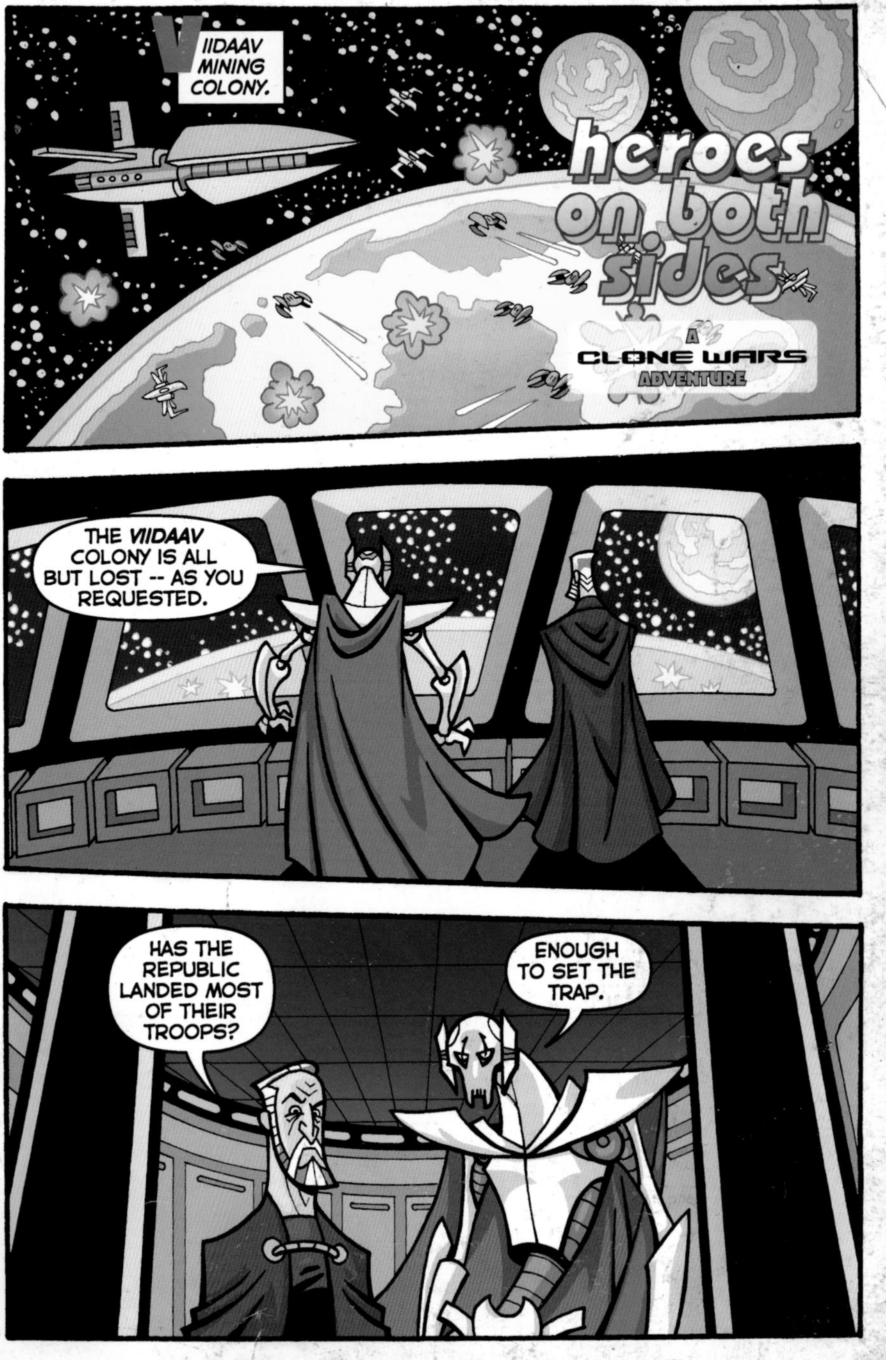
VIIDAAV MINING COLONY.
heroes on both sides
A CLONE WARS ADVENTURE
THE VIIDAAV COLONY IS ALL BUT LOST -- AS YOU REQUESTED.
HAS THE REPUBLIC LANDED MOST OF THEIR TROOPS?
ENOUGH TO SET THE TRAP.

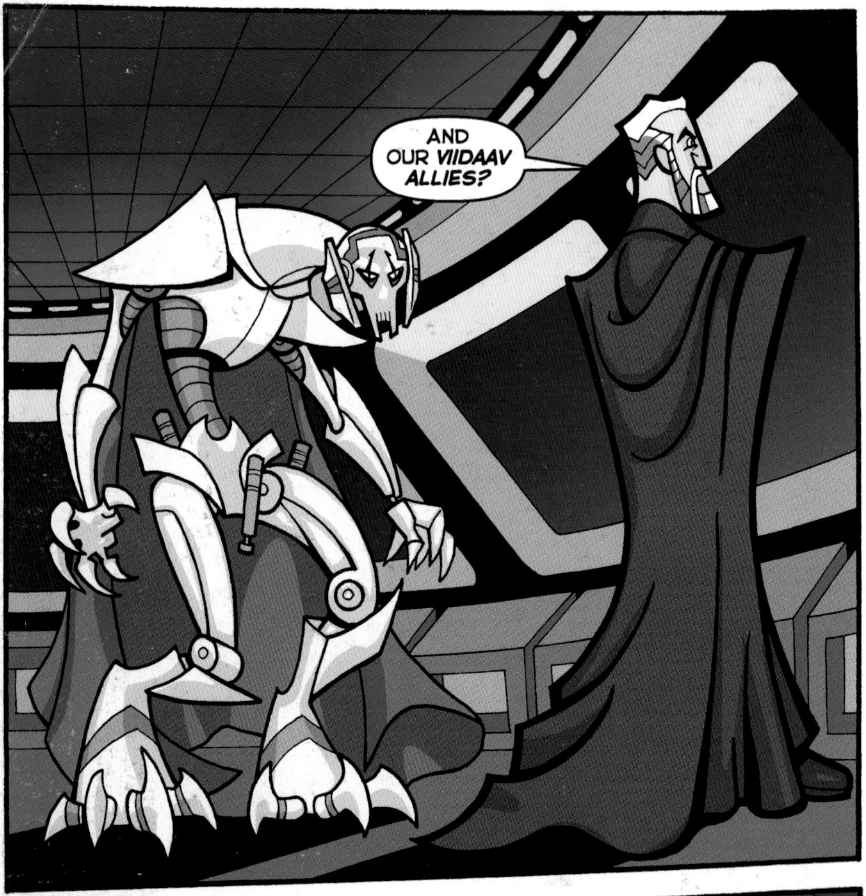
AND OUR *VIIDAAV ALLIES?*

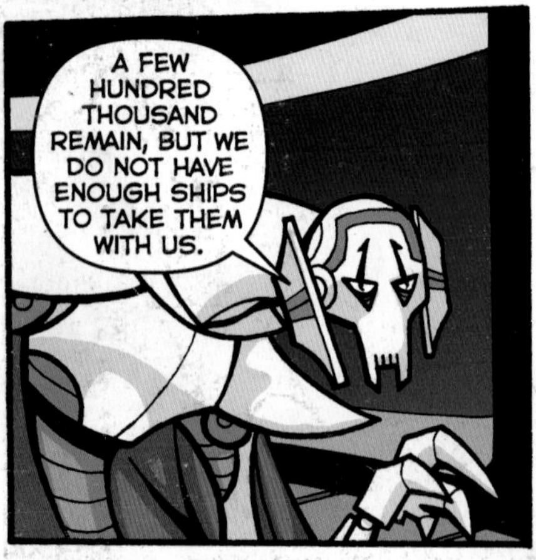
A FEW HUNDRED THOUSAND REMAIN, BUT WE DO NOT HAVE ENOUGH SHIPS TO TAKE THEM WITH US.

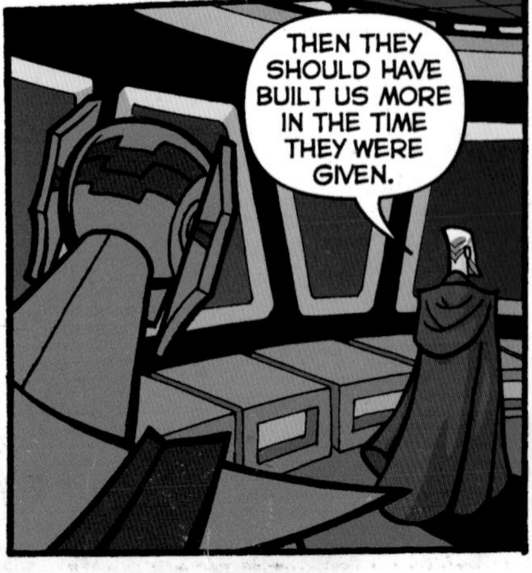
THEN THEY SHOULD HAVE BUILT US MORE IN THE TIME THEY WERE GIVEN.

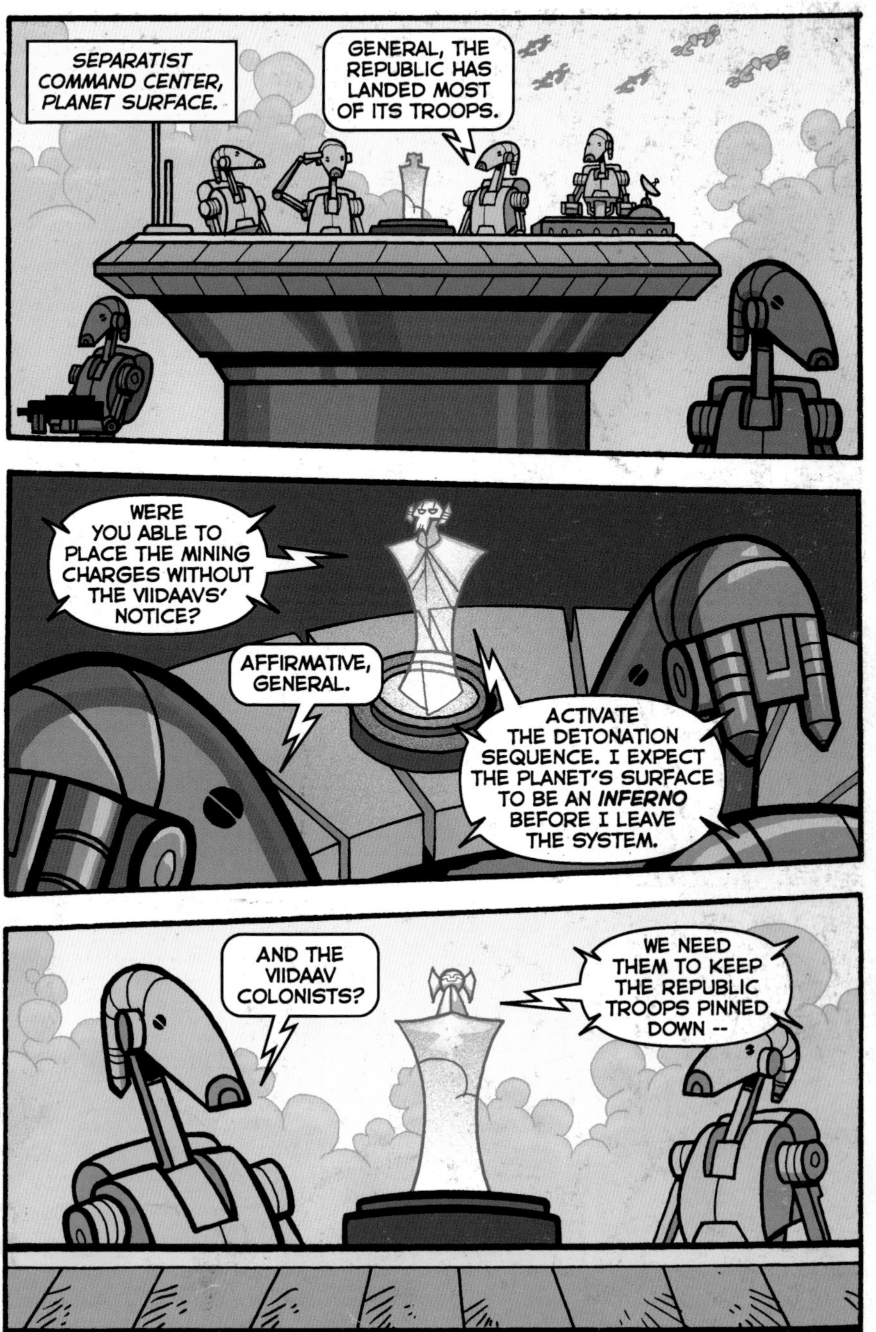
SEPARATIST COMMAND CENTER, PLANET SURFACE.
GENERAL, THE REPUBLIC HAS LANDED MOST OF ITS TROOPS.
WERE YOU ABLE TO PLACE THE MINING CHARGES WITHOUT THE VIIDAAVS' NOTICE?
AFFIRMATIVE, GENERAL.
ACTIVATE THE DETONATION SEQUENCE. I EXPECT THE PLANET'S SURFACE TO BE AN *INFERNO* BEFORE I LEAVE THE SYSTEM.
AND THE VIIDAAV COLONISTS?
WE NEED THEM TO KEEP THE REPUBLIC TROOPS PINNED DOWN --

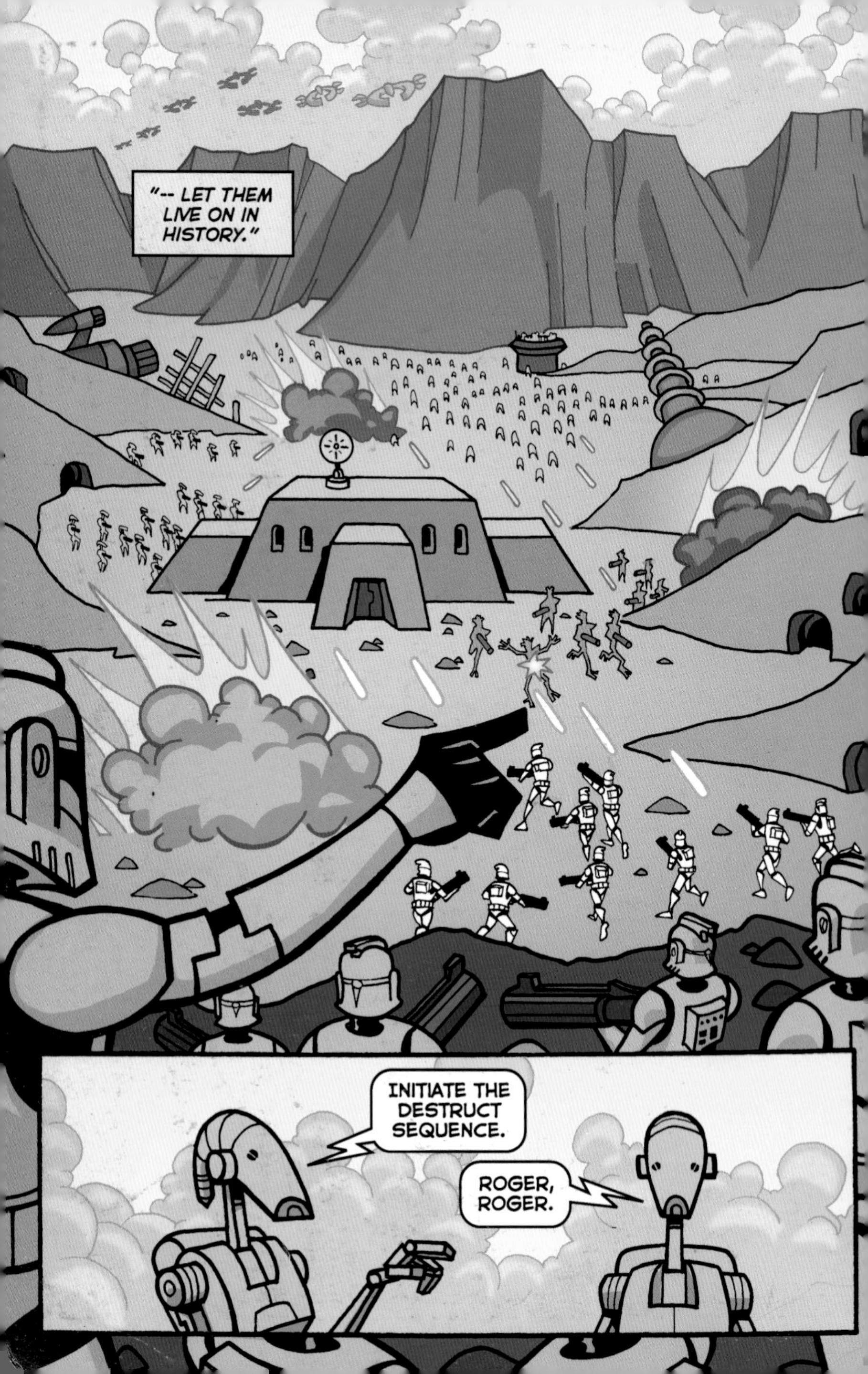
"-- LET THEM LIVE ON IN HISTORY."
INITIATE THE DESTRUCT SEQUENCE.
ROGER, ROGER.

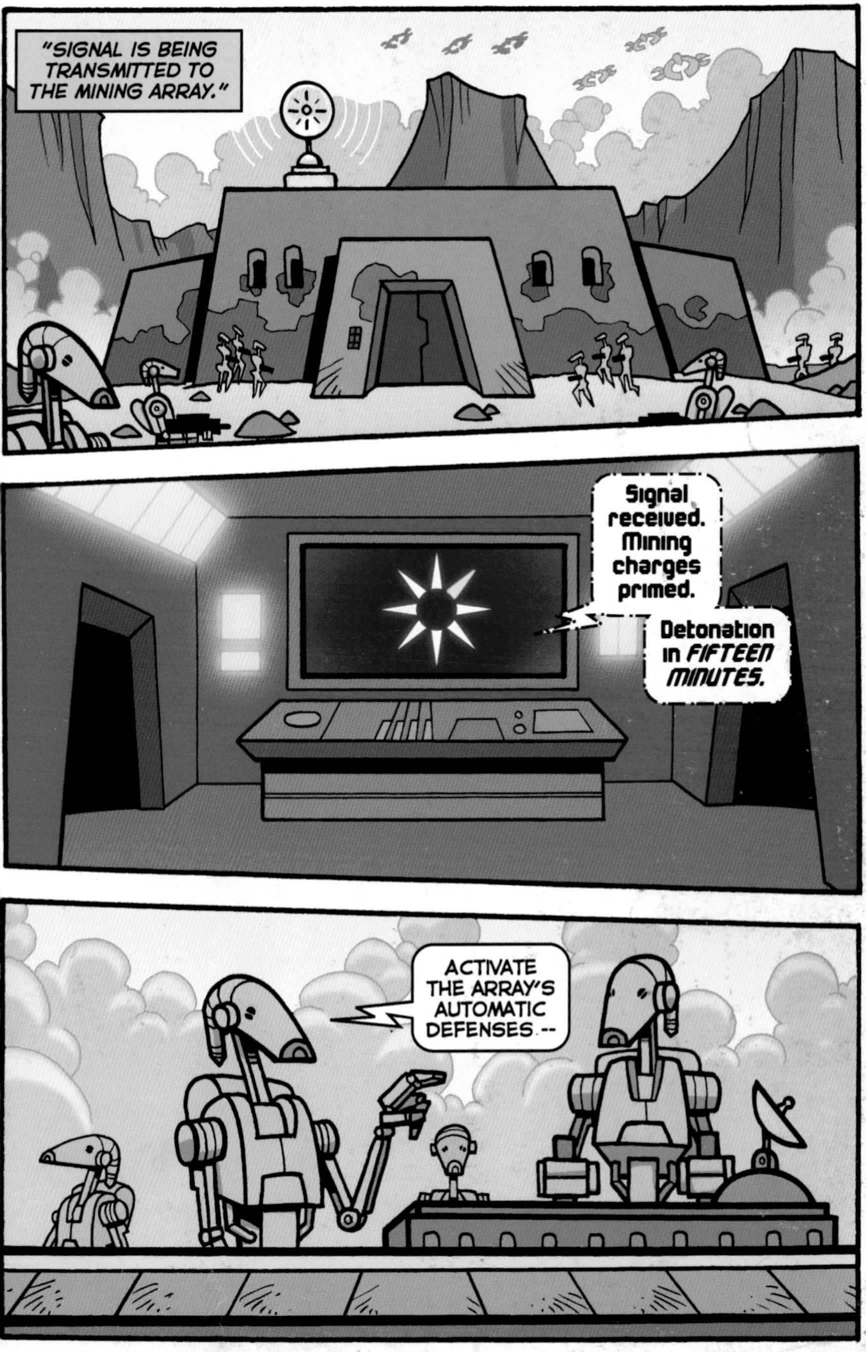
"SIGNAL IS BEING TRANSMITTED TO THE MINING ARRAY."
Signal received. Mining charges primed.
Detonation in *FIFTEEN MINUTES.*
ACTIVATE THE ARRAY'S AUTOMATIC DEFENSES --

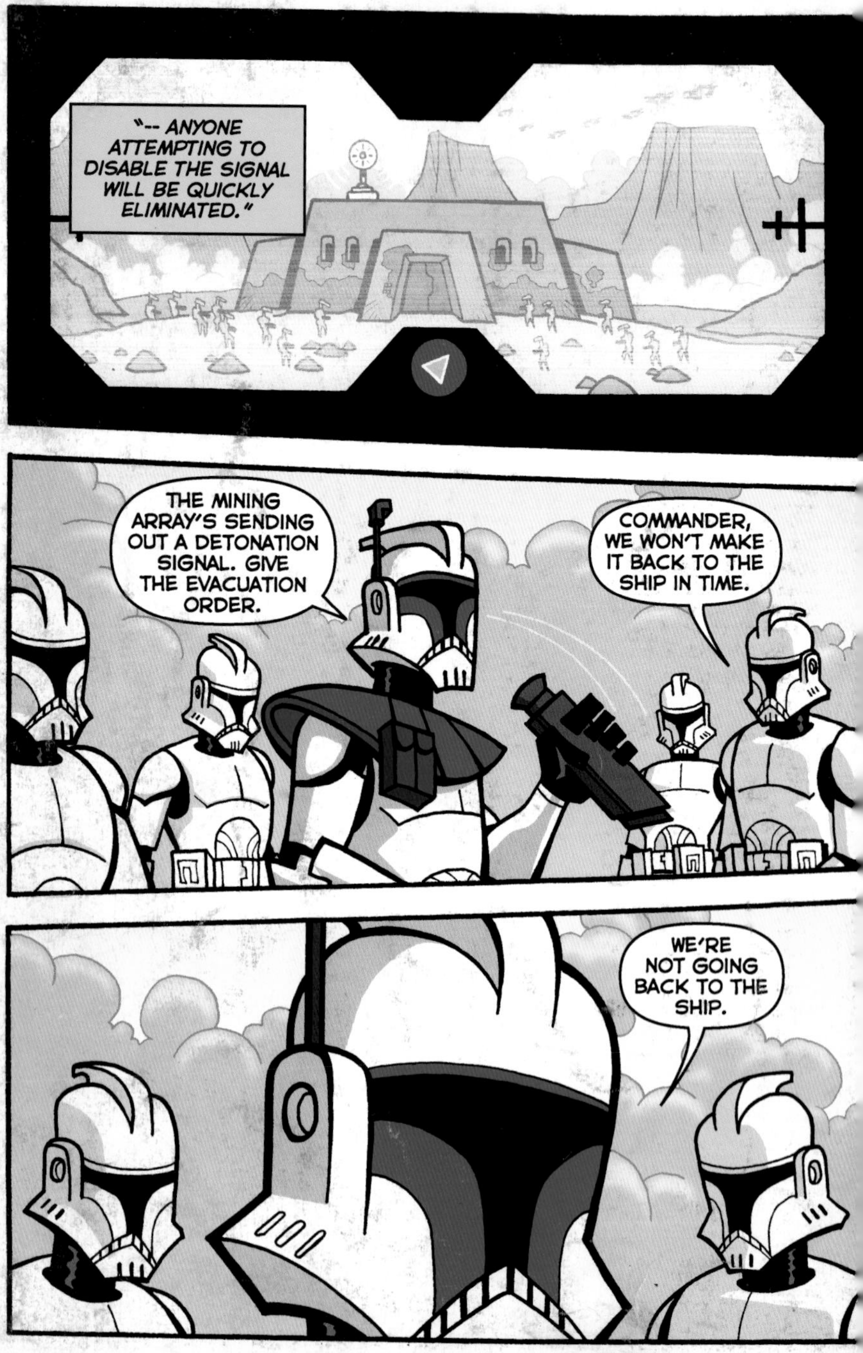
"-- ANYONE ATTEMPTING TO DISABLE THE SIGNAL WILL BE QUICKLY ELIMINATED."
THE MINING ARRAY'S SENDING OUT A DETONATION SIGNAL. GIVE THE EVACUATION ORDER.
COMMANDER, WE WON'T MAKE IT BACK TO THE SHIP IN TIME.
WE'RE NOT GOING BACK TO THE SHIP.

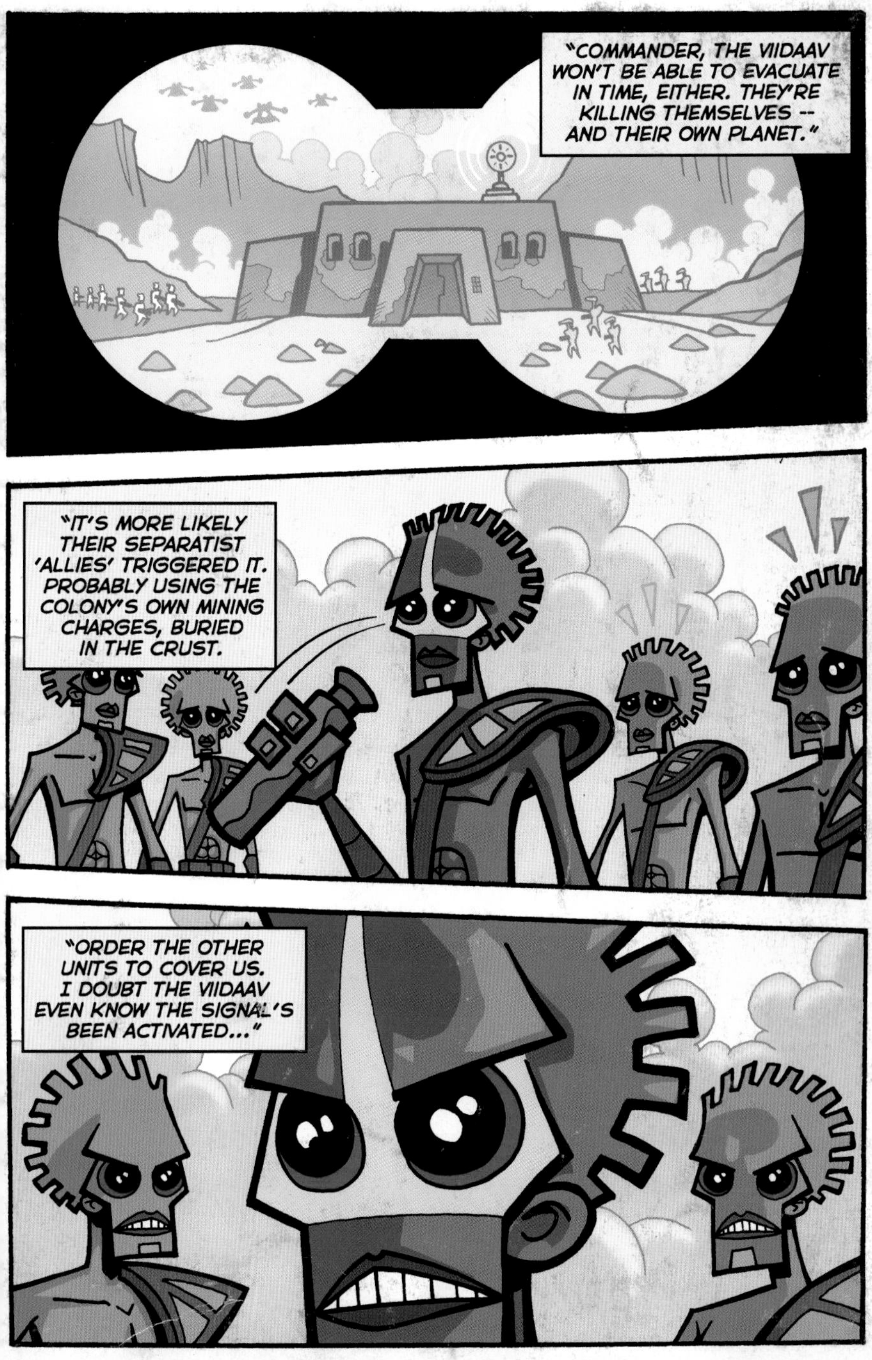
"COMMANDER, THE VIIDAAV WON'T BE ABLE TO EVACUATE IN TIME, EITHER. THEY'RE KILLING THEMSELVES -- AND THEIR OWN PLANET."
"IT'S MORE LIKELY THEIR SEPARATIST 'ALLIES' TRIGGERED IT. PROBABLY USING THE COLONY'S OWN MINING CHARGES, BURIED IN THE CRUST.
"ORDER THE OTHER UNITS TO COVER US. I DOUBT THE VIIDAAV EVEN KNOW THE SIGNAL'S BEEN ACTIVATED..."

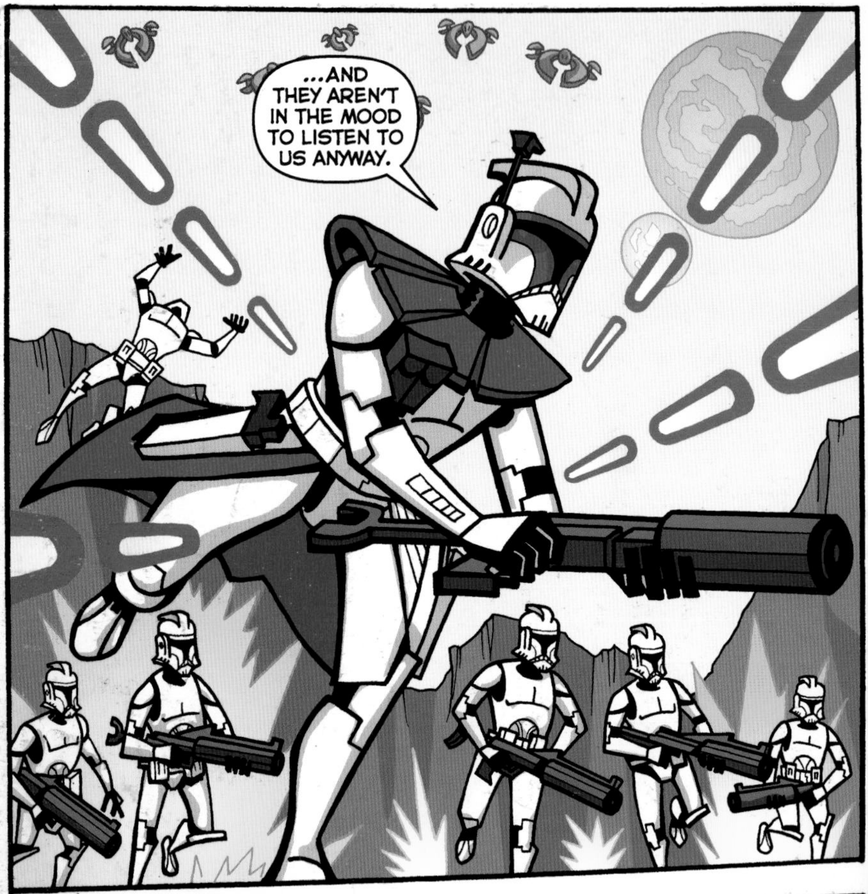
...AND THEY AREN'T IN THE MOOD TO LISTEN TO US ANYWAY.

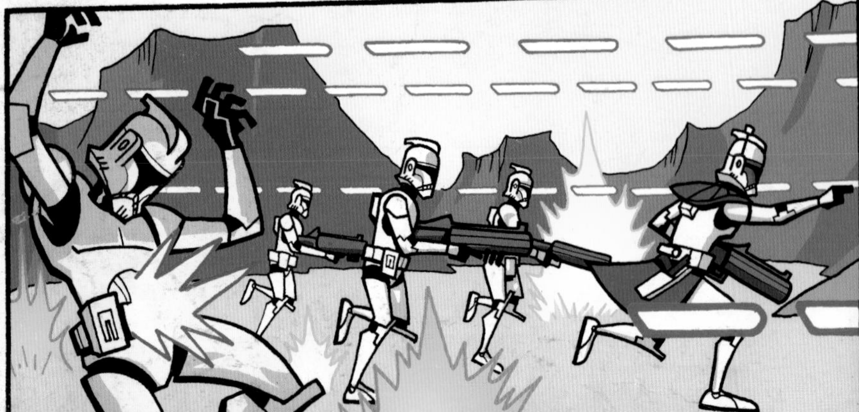

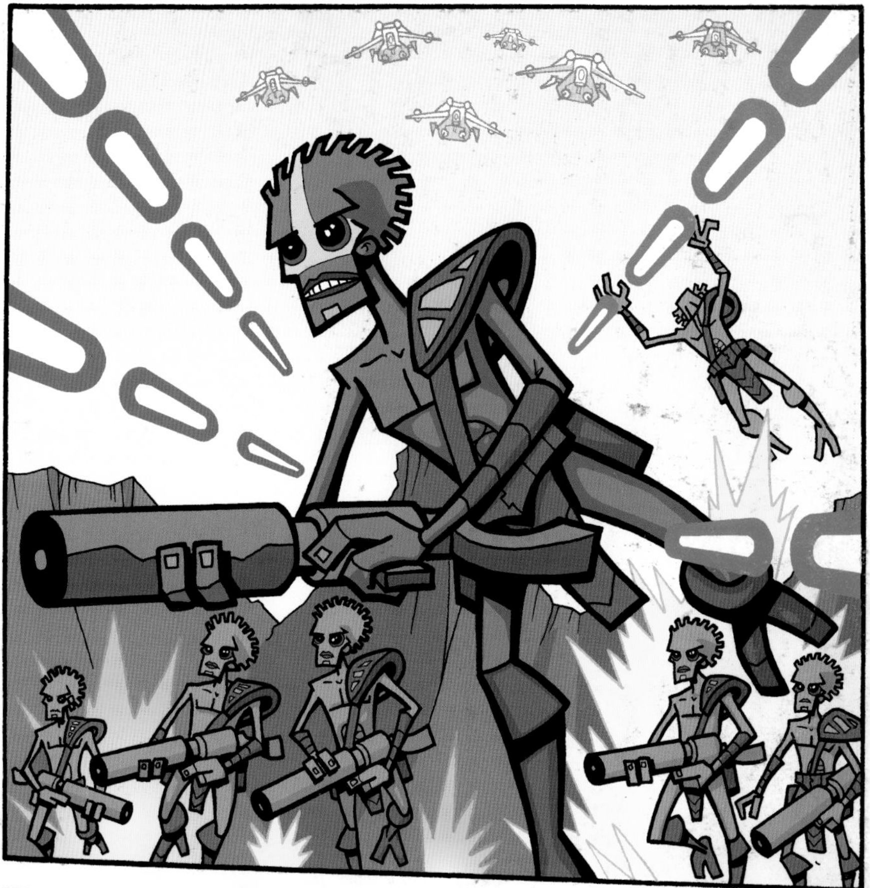

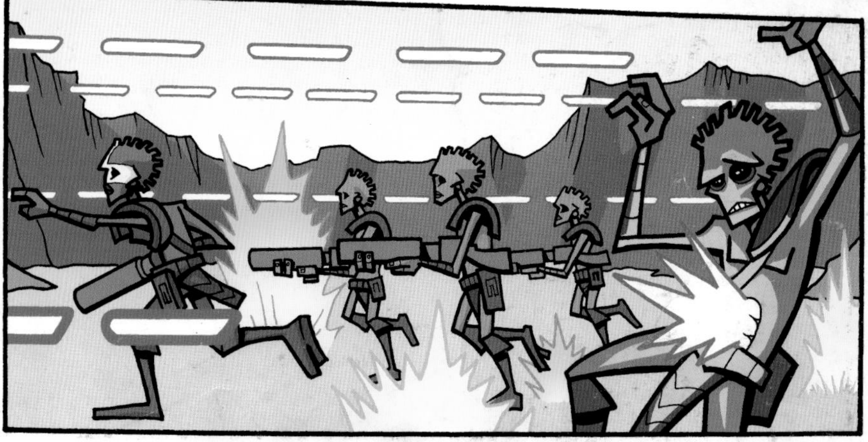

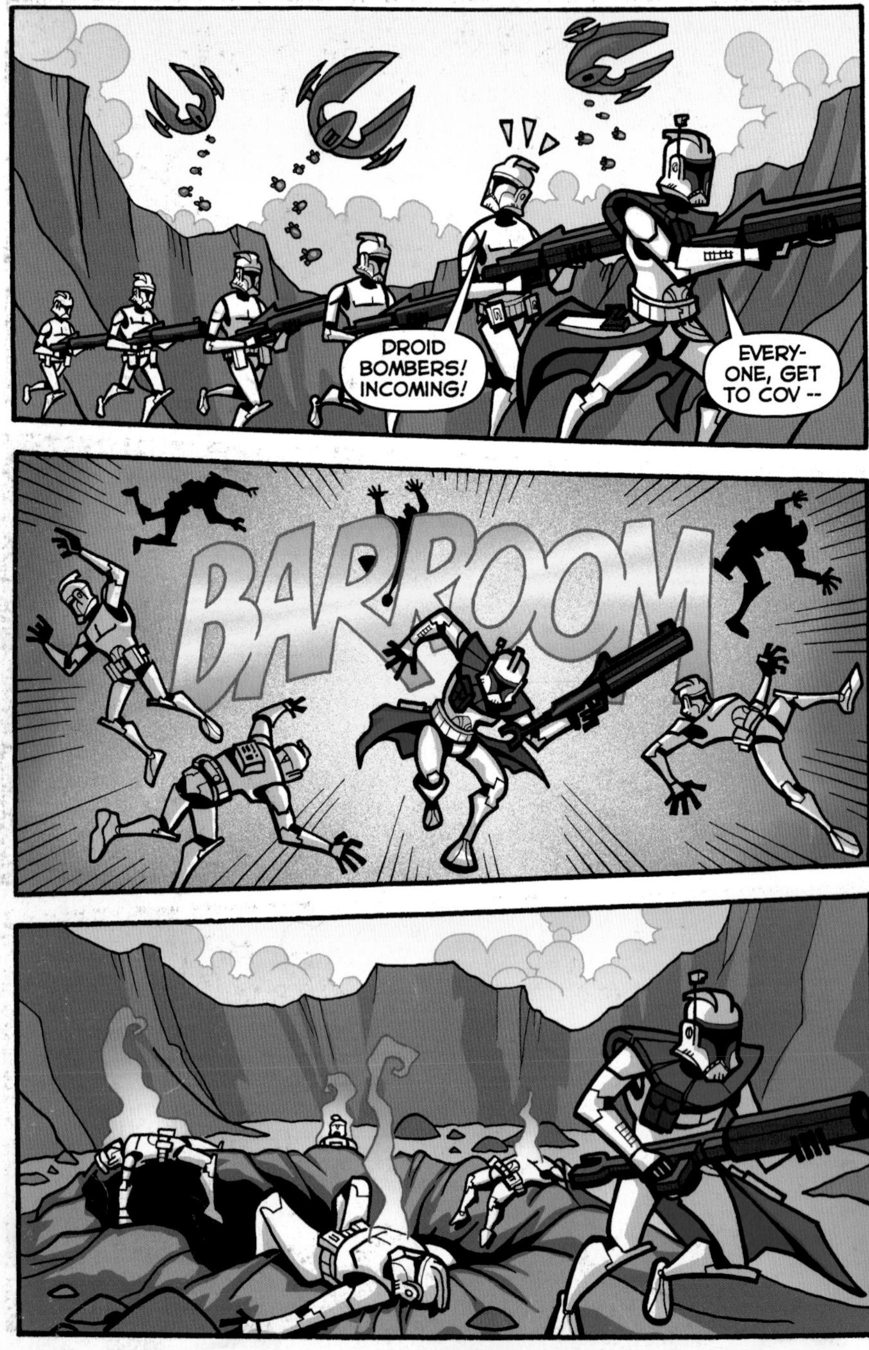
DROID BOMBERS! INCOMING!
EVERY-ONE, GET TO COV --
BARROOM

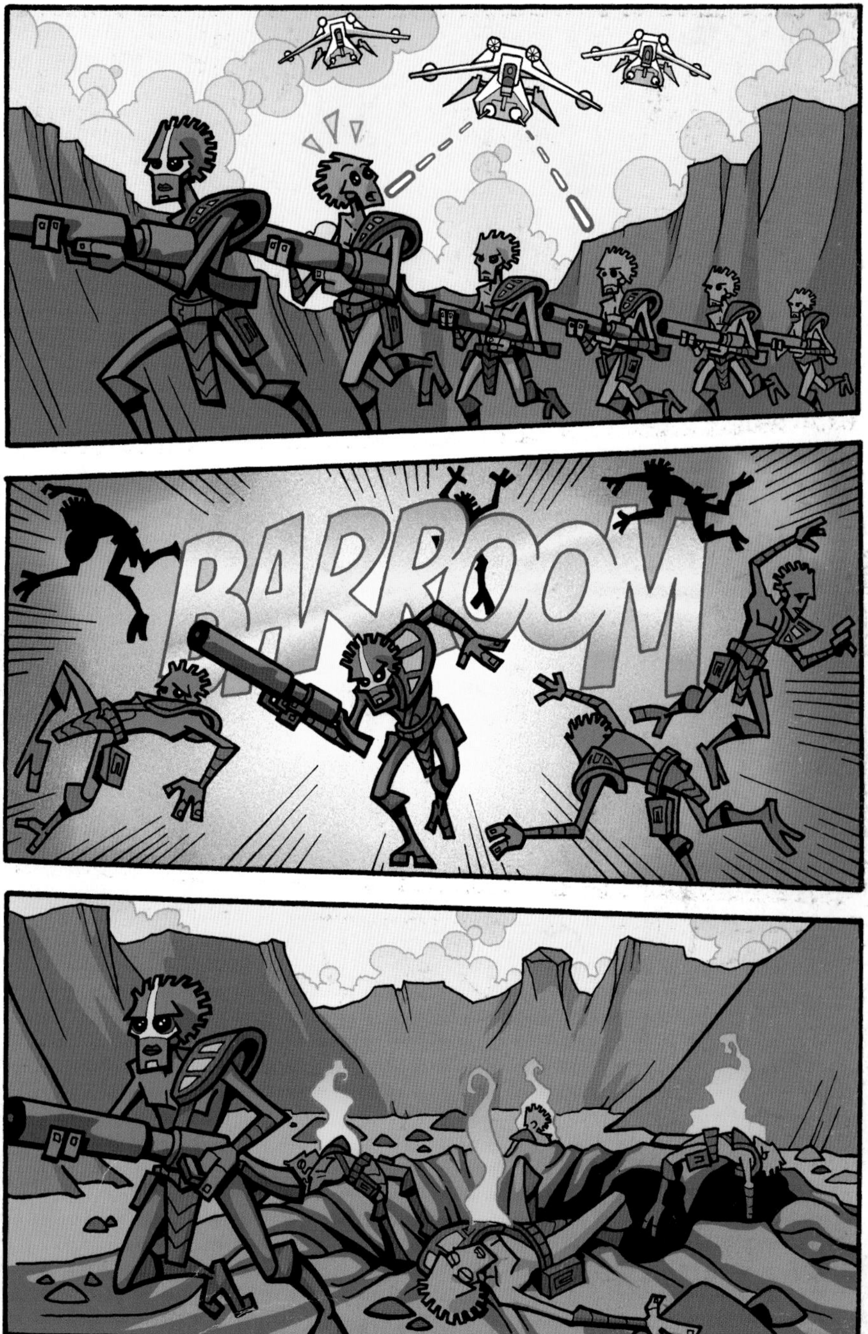
BARROOM

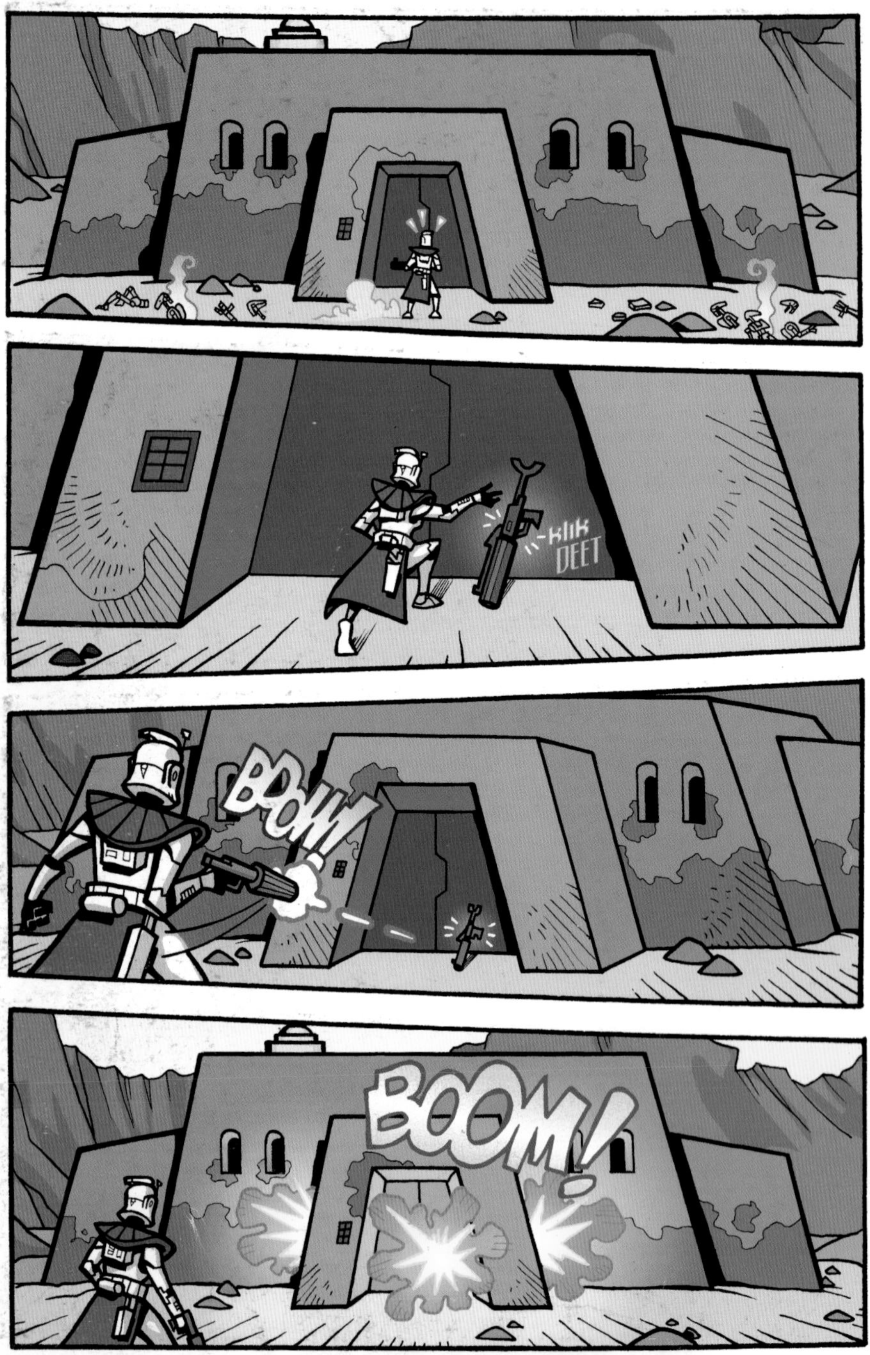
KLIK
DEET
BDOW
BOOM!

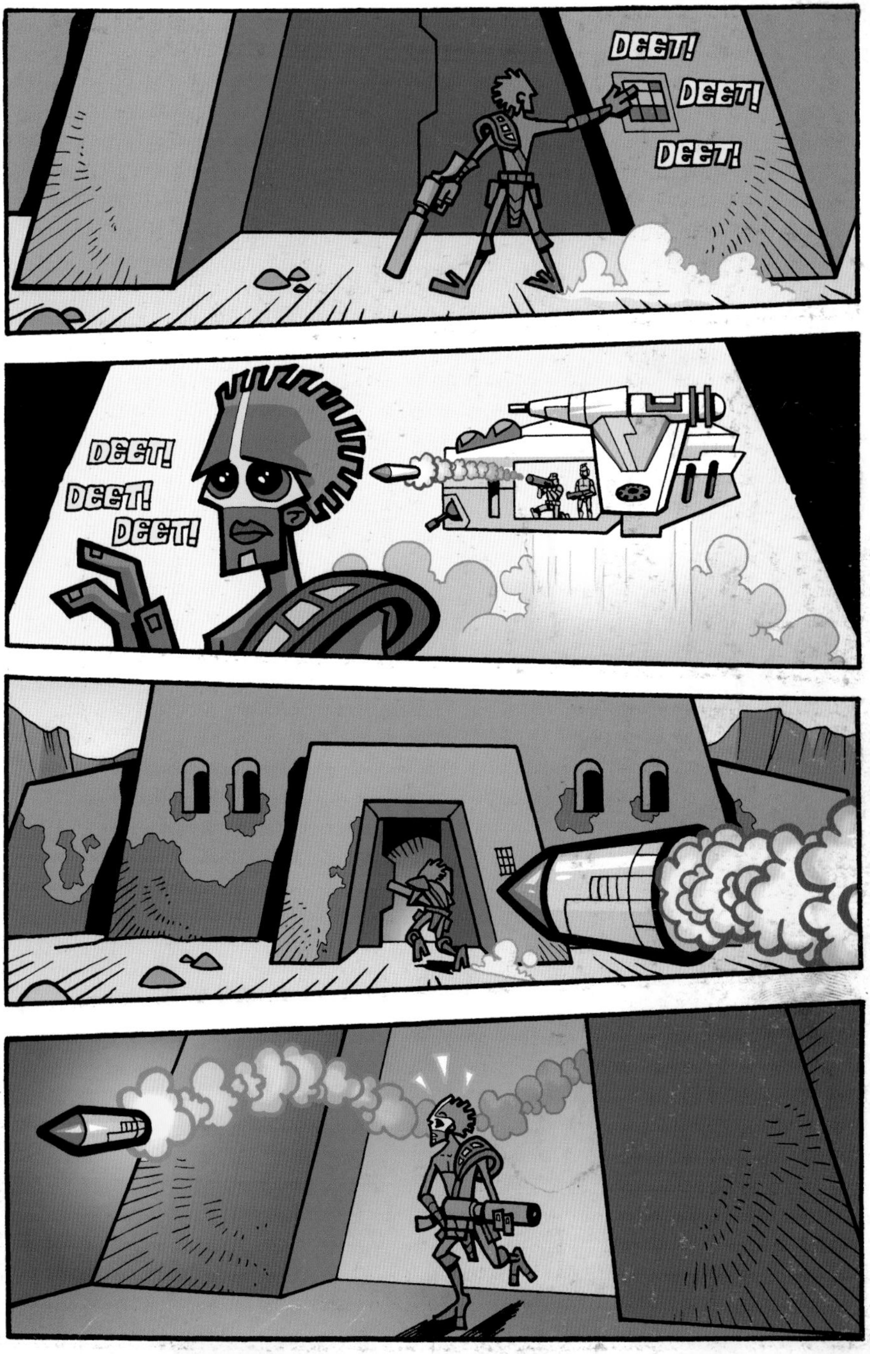
DEET!
DEET!
DEET!
DEET!
DEET!
DEET!

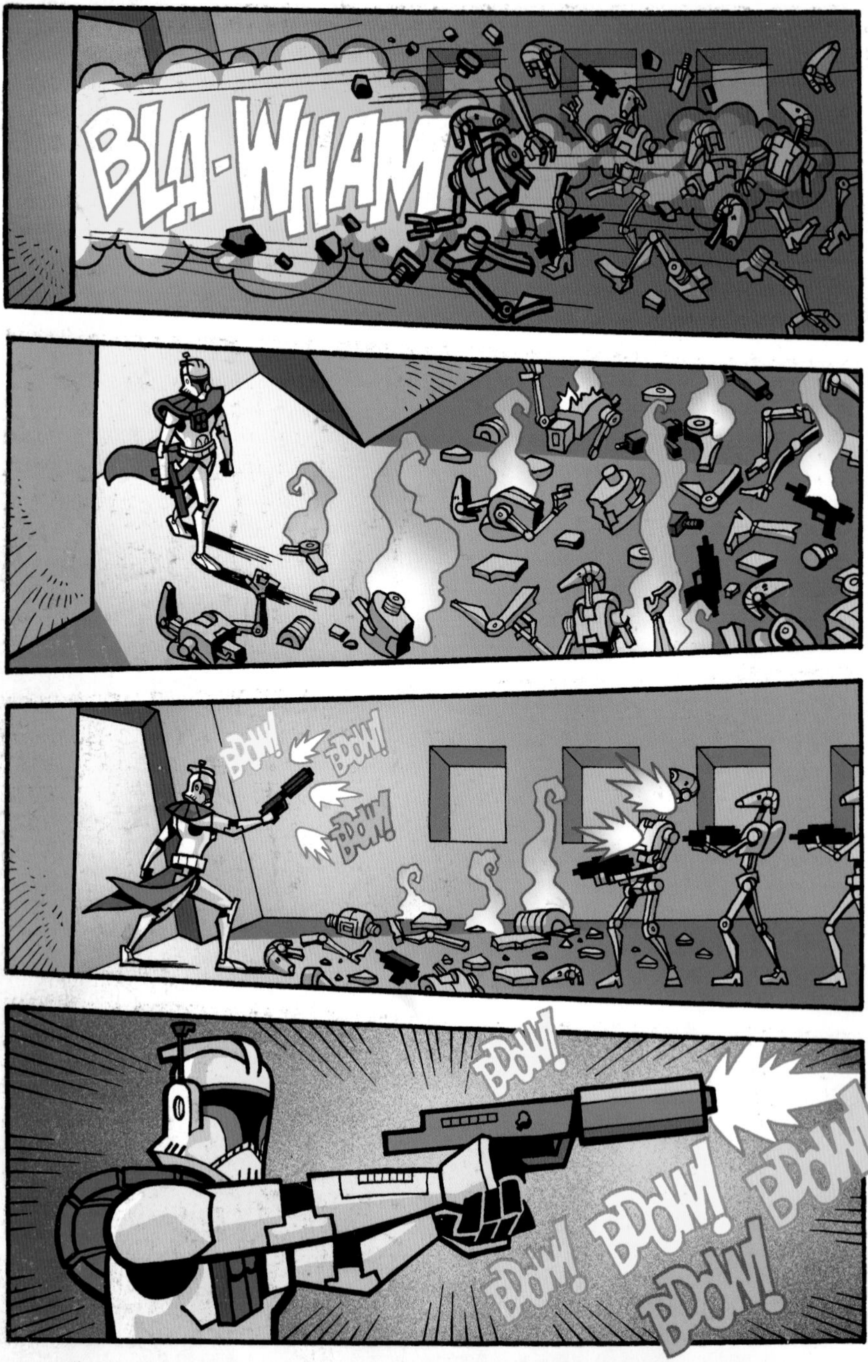
BLA-WHAM
BDOW!
BDOW!
BDOW!
BDOW!
BDOW!
BDOW!
BDOW!
BDOW!
BDOW!

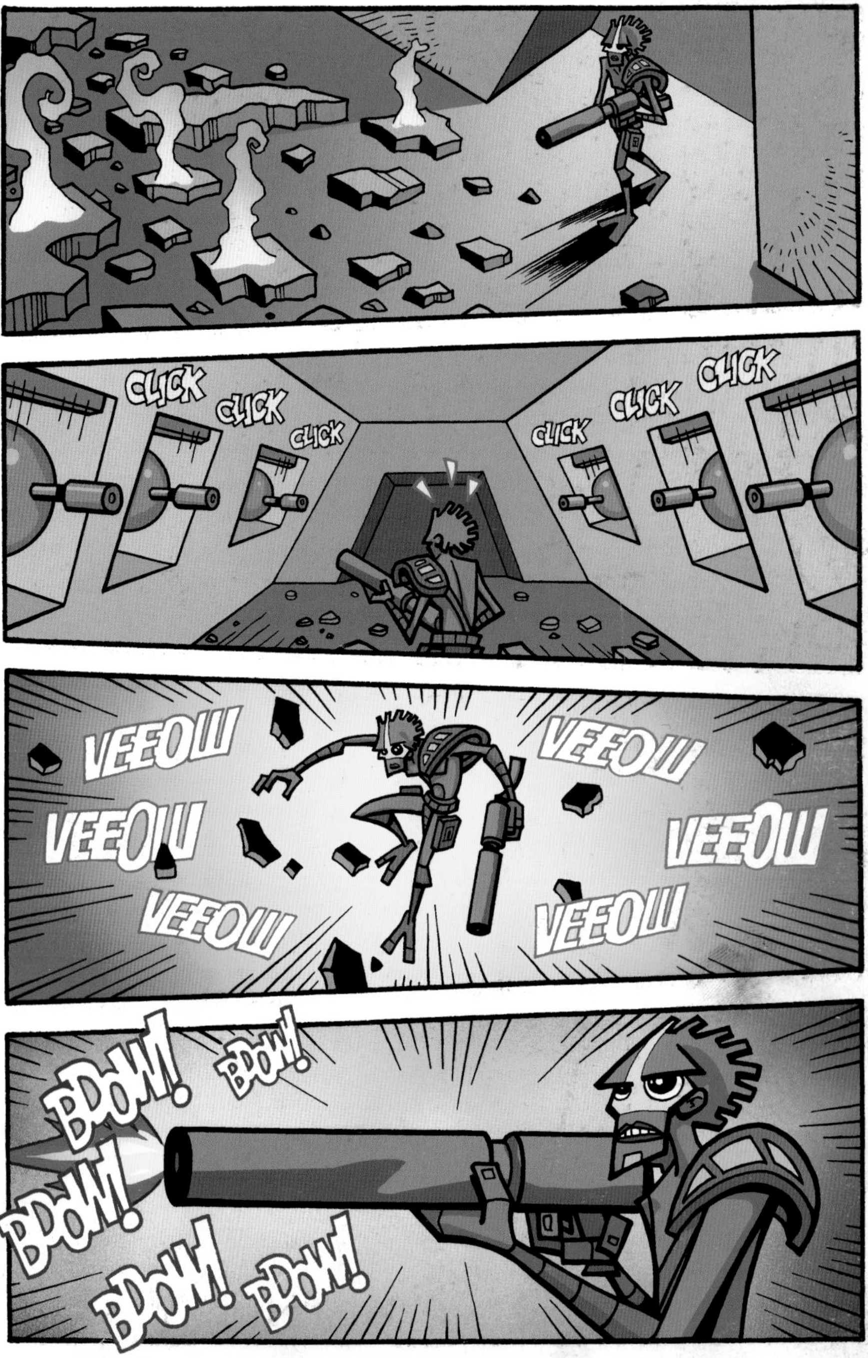
CLICK
CLICK
CLICK
CLICK
CLICK
CLICK
VEEOW
VEEOW
VEEOW
VEEOW
VEEOW
VEEOW
BDOW!
BDOW!
BDOW!
BDOW!
BDOW!

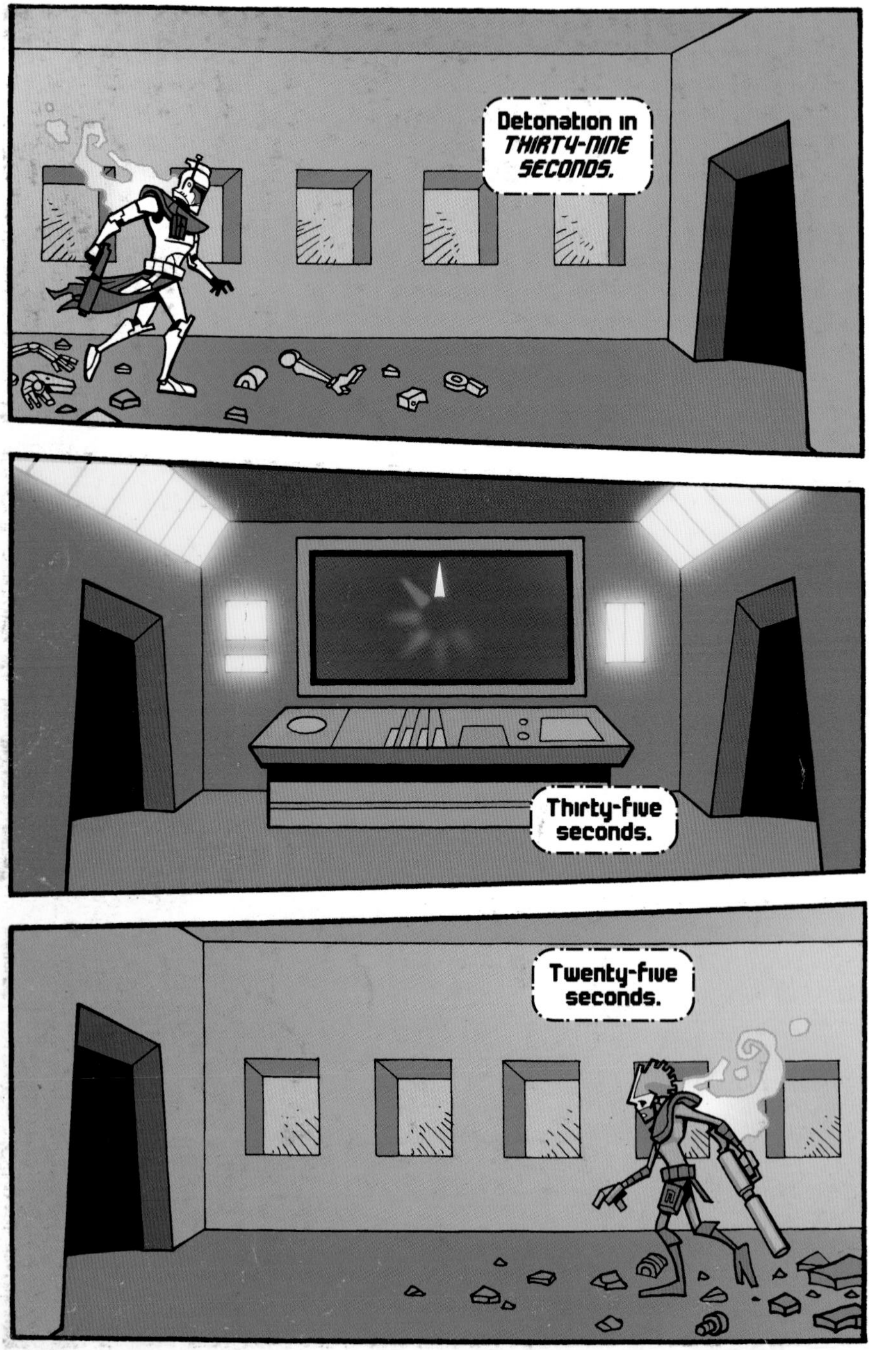
Detonation in THIRTY-NINE SECONDS.
Thirty-five seconds.
Twenty-five seconds.

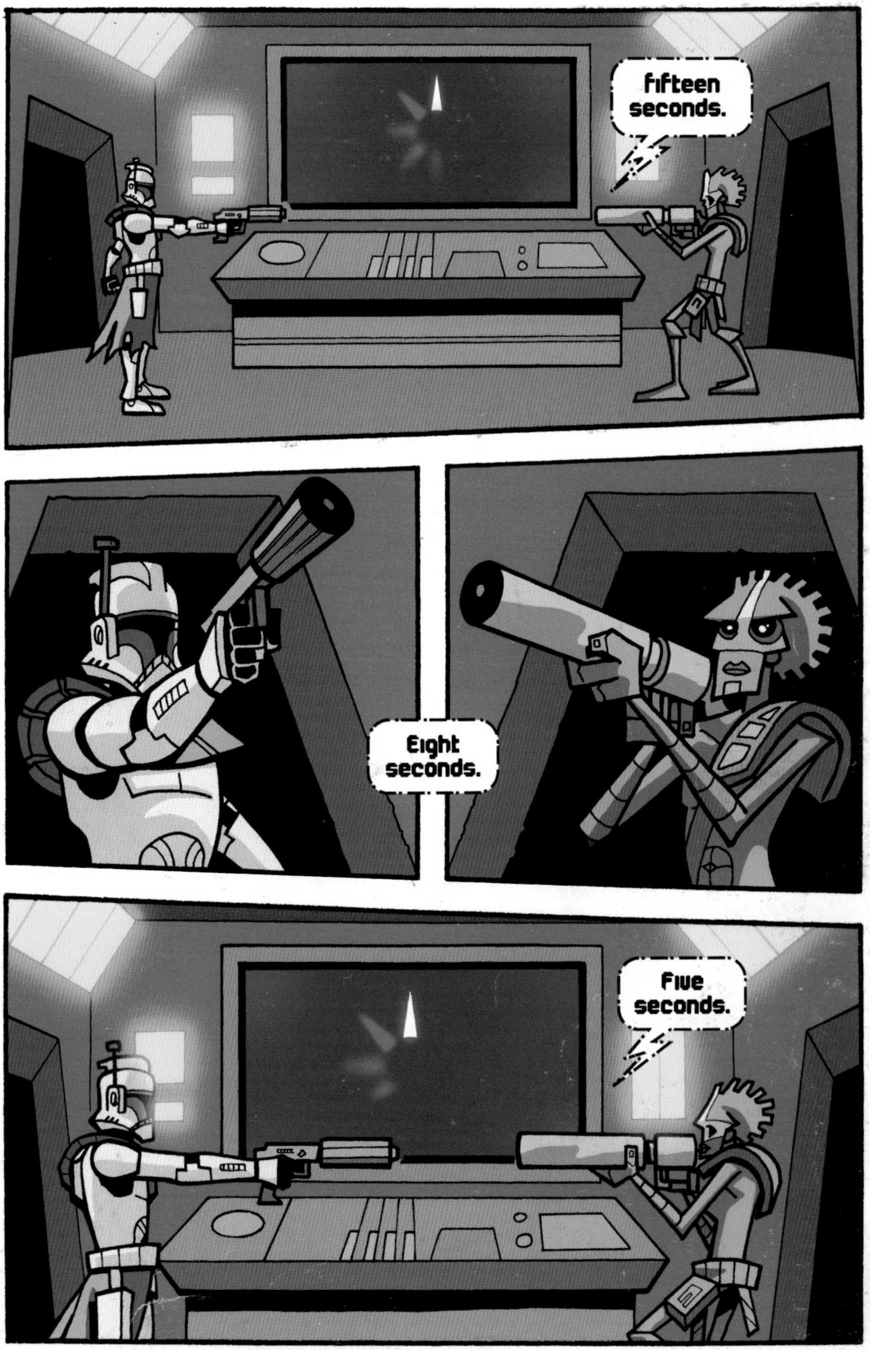
fifteen seconds.
Eight seconds.
Five seconds.

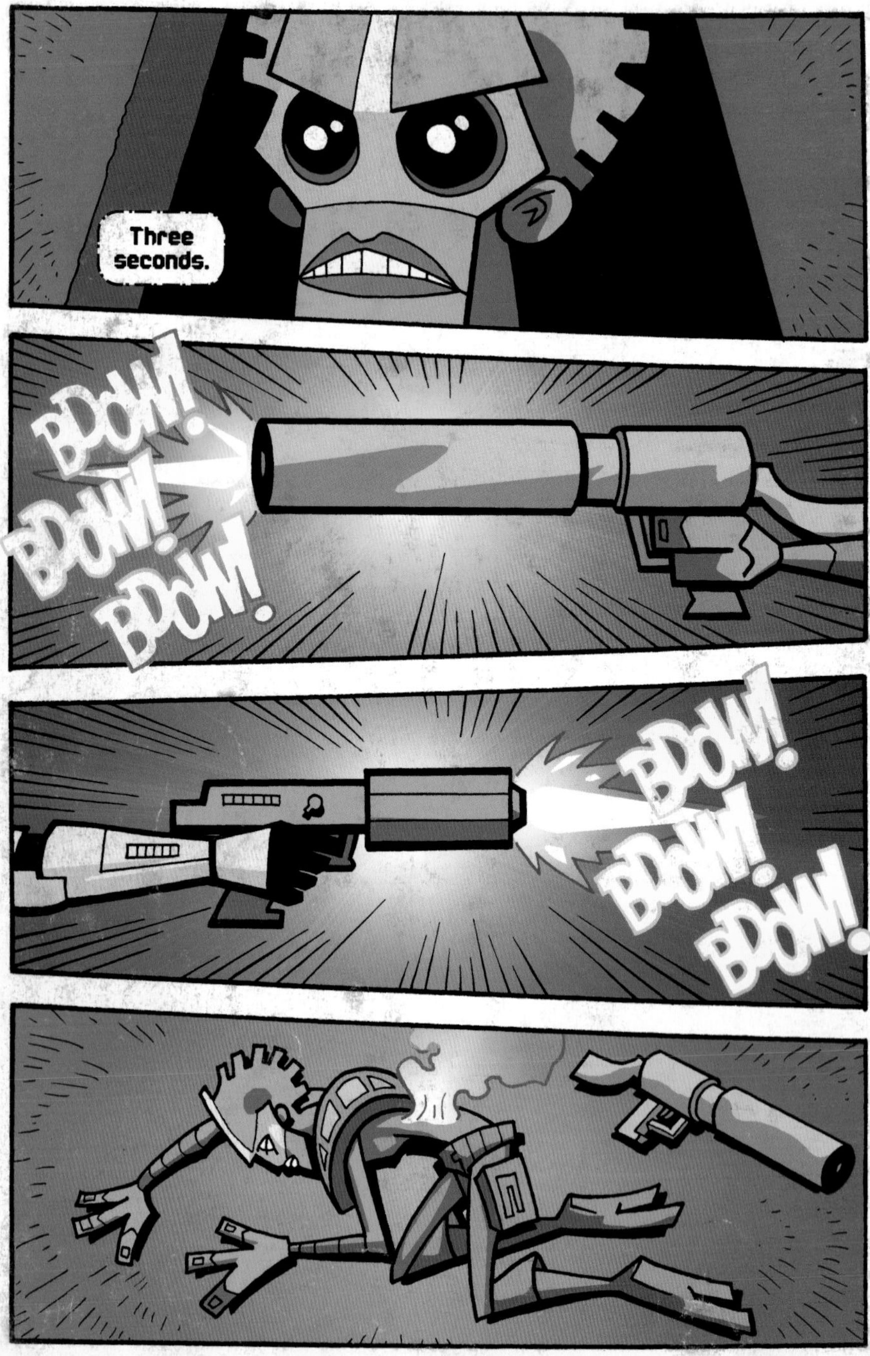
Three seconds.
BDOW! BDOW! BDOW!
BDOW! BDOW! BDOW!

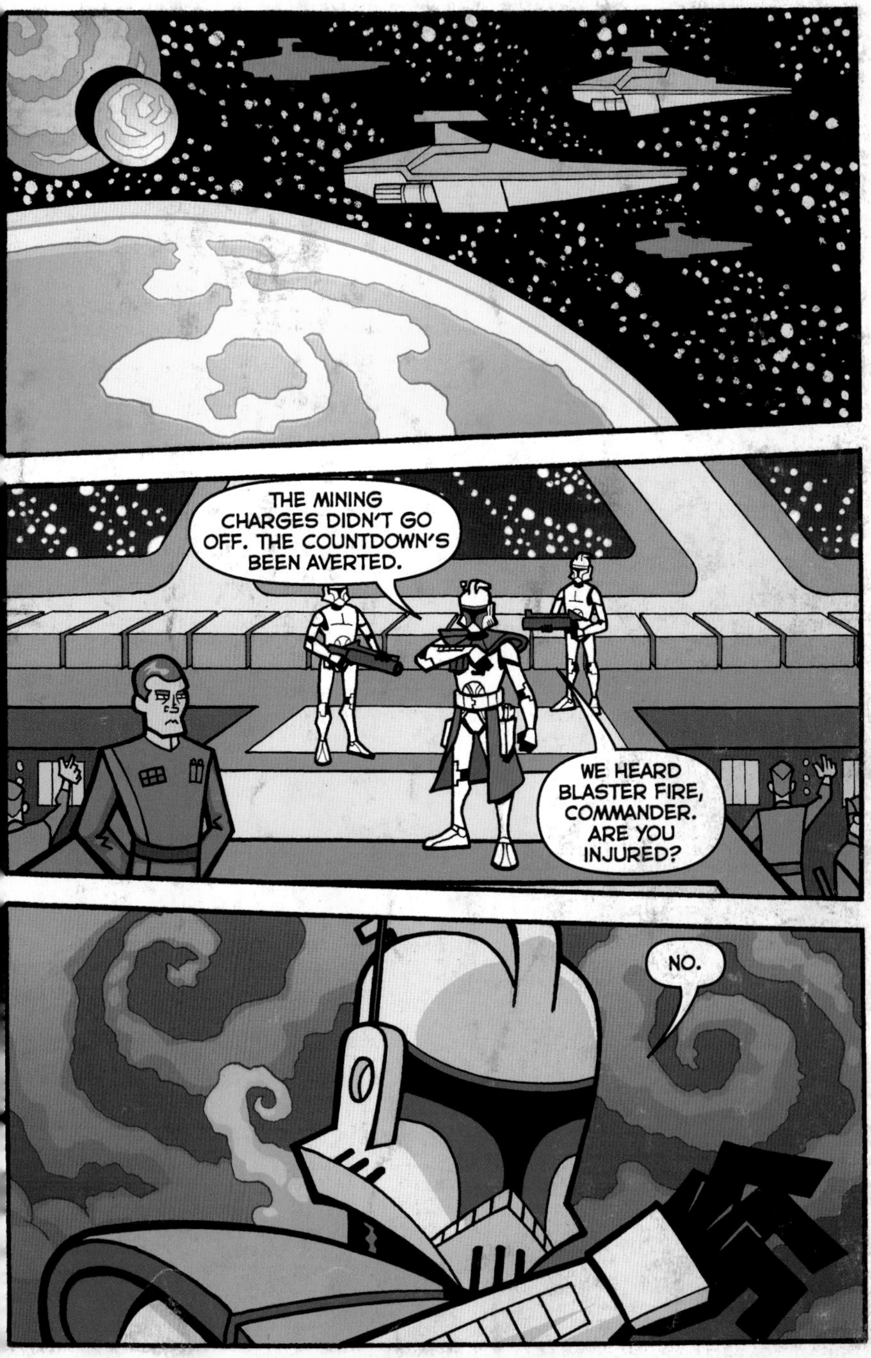
THE MINING CHARGES DIDN'T GO OFF. THE COUNTDOWN'S BEEN AVERTED.
WE HEARD BLASTER FIRE, COMMANDER. ARE YOU INJURED?
NO.

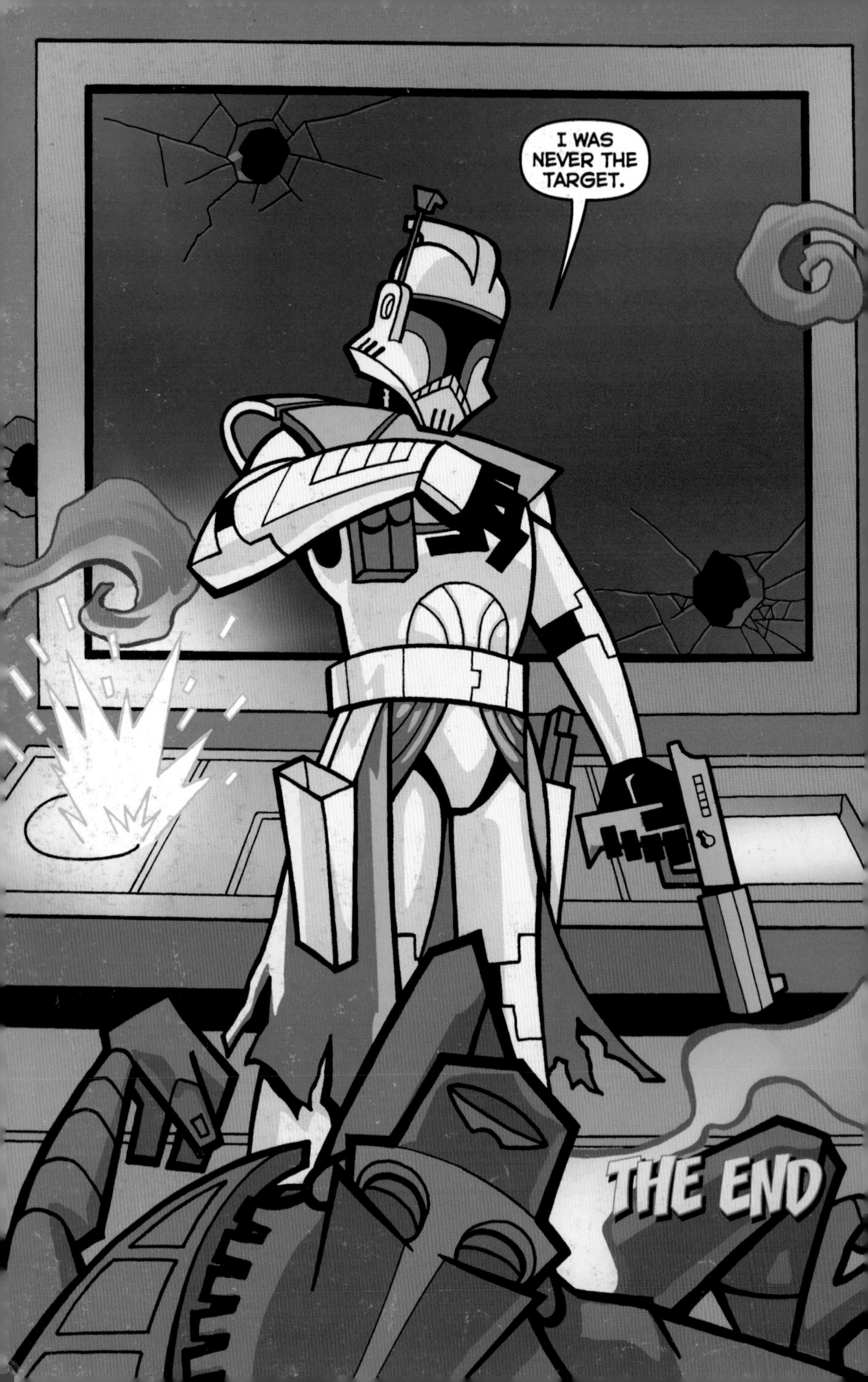
I WAS NEVER THE TARGET.
THE END

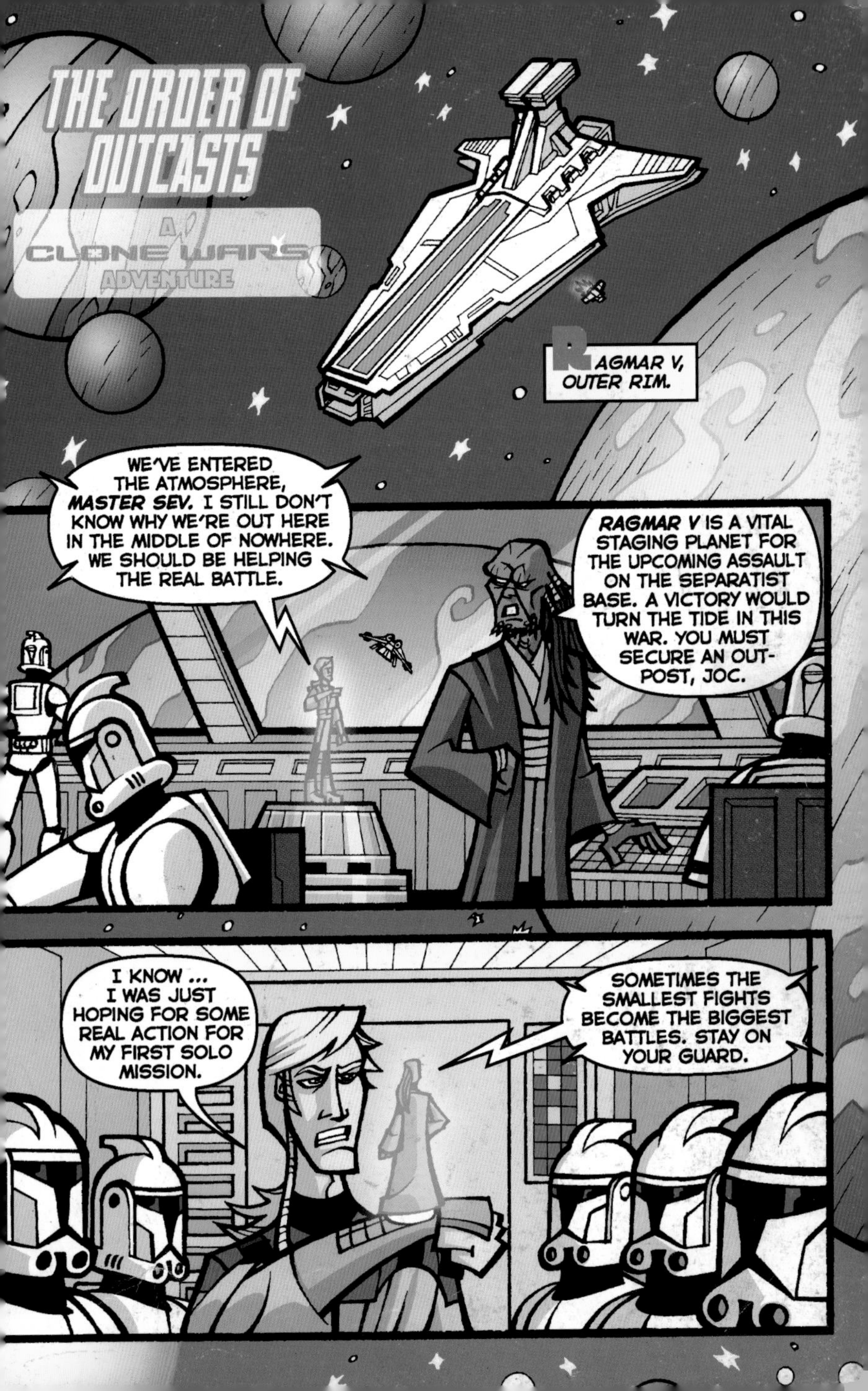
THE ORDER OF OUTCASTS
A CLONE WARS ADVENTURE
RAGMAR V, OUTER RIM.
WE'VE ENTERED THE ATMOSPHERE, MASTER SEV. I STILL DON'T KNOW WHY WE'RE OUT HERE IN THE MIDDLE OF NOWHERE. WE SHOULD BE HELPING THE REAL BATTLE.
RAGMAR V IS A VITAL STAGING PLANET FOR THE UPCOMING ASSAULT ON THE SEPARATIST BASE. A VICTORY WOULD TURN THE TIDE IN THIS WAR. YOU MUST SECURE AN OUT-POST, JOC.
I KNOW ... I WAS JUST HOPING FOR SOME REAL ACTION FOR MY FIRST SOLO MISSION.
SOMETIMES THE SMALLEST FIGHTS BECOME THE BIGGEST BATTLES. STAY ON YOUR GUARD.

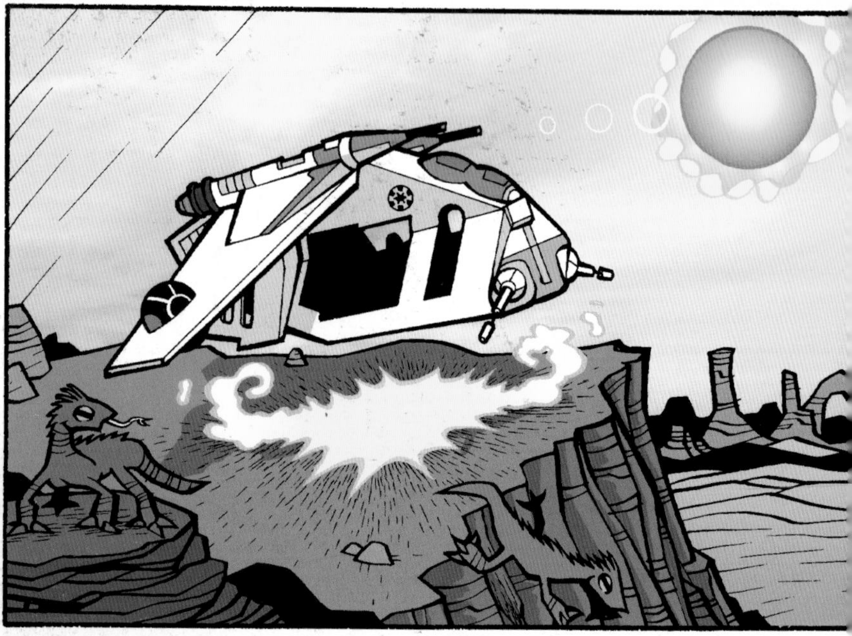

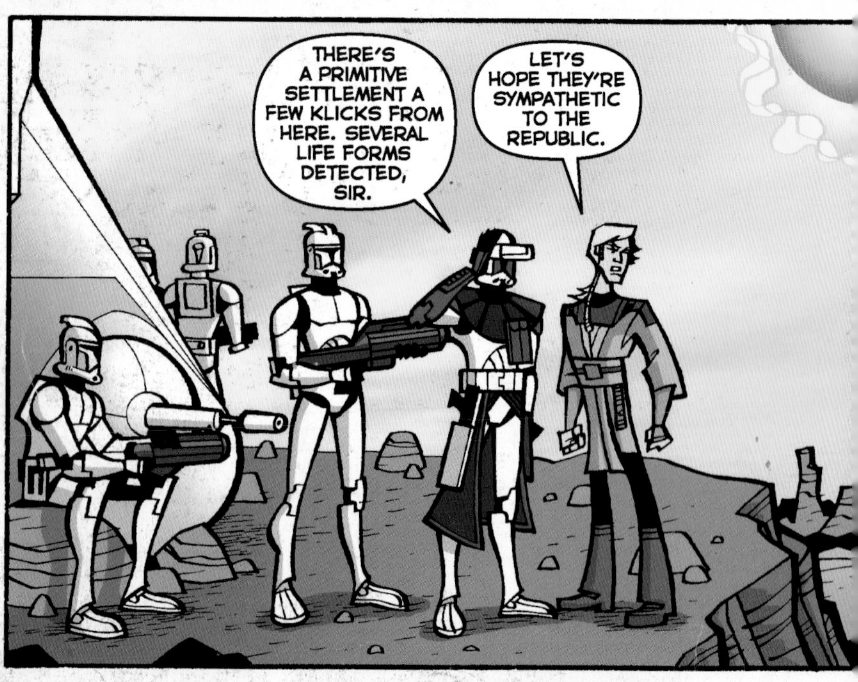
THERE'S A PRIMITIVE SETTLEMENT A FEW KLICKS FROM HERE. SEVERAL LIFE FORMS DETECTED, SIR.
LET'S HOPE THEY'RE SYMPATHETIC TO THE REPUBLIC.

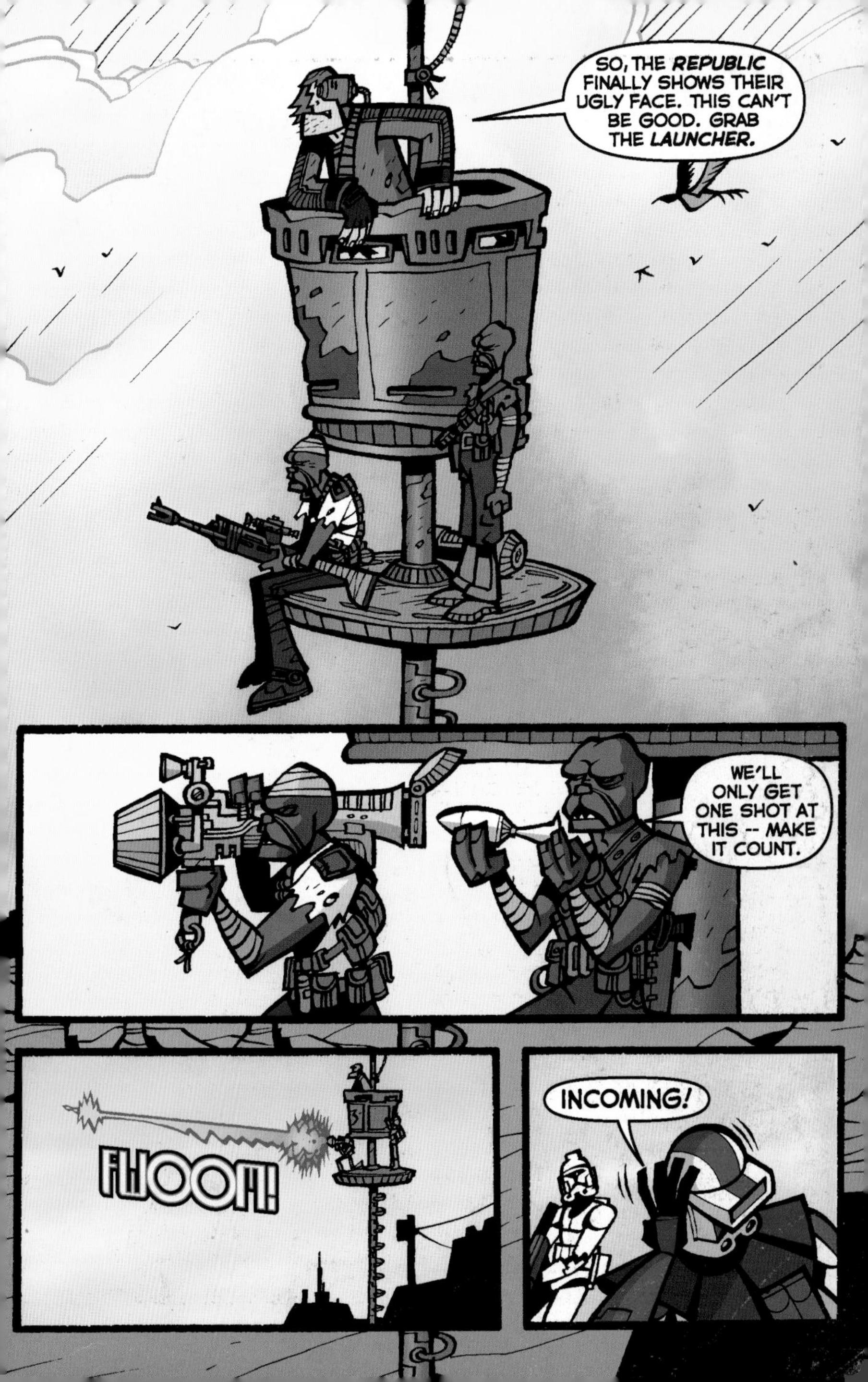
SO, THE REPUBLIC FINALLY SHOWS THEIR UGLY FACE. THIS CAN'T BE GOOD. GRAB THE LAUNCHER.
WE'LL ONLY GET ONE SHOT AT THIS -- MAKE IT COUNT.
FWOOM!
INCOMING!

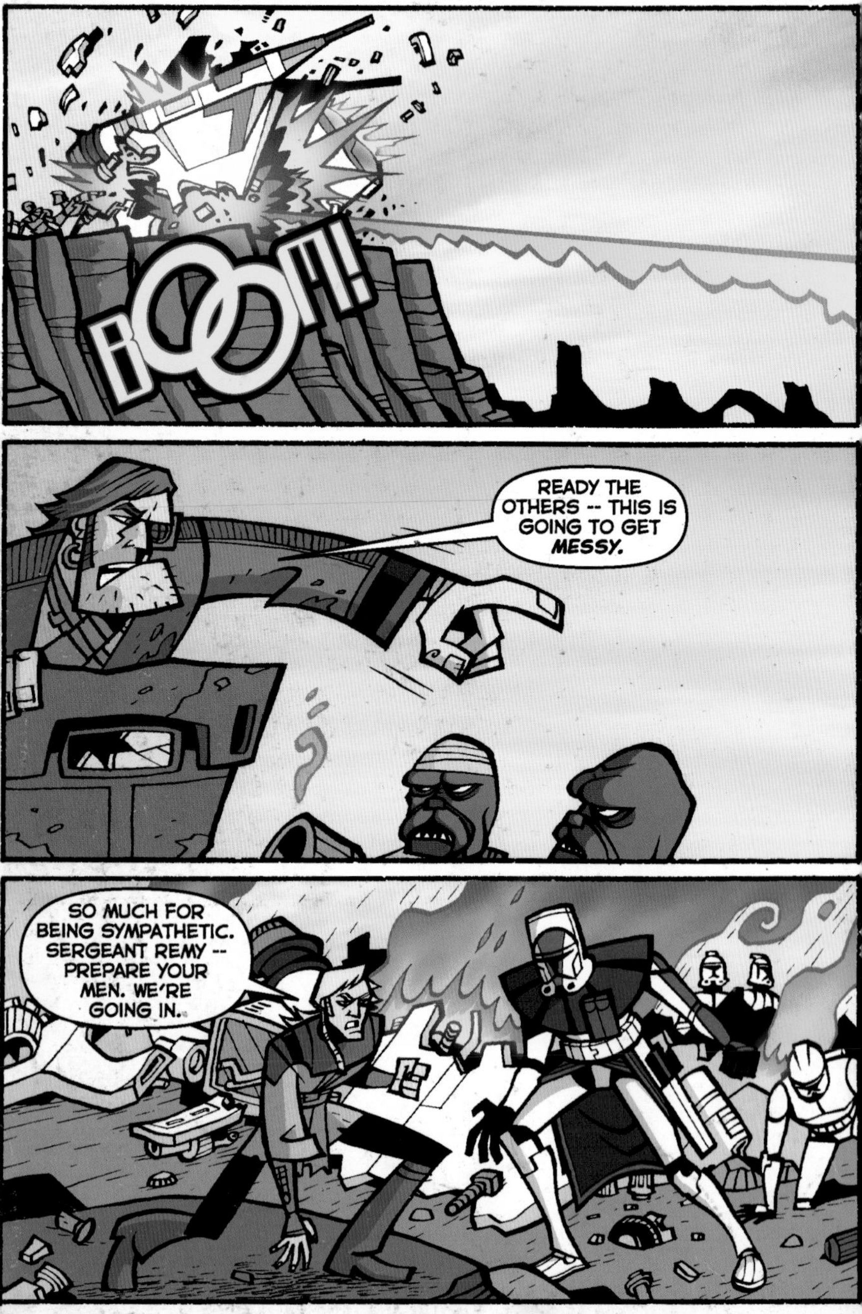
BOOM!
READY THE OTHERS -- THIS IS GOING TO GET *MESSY.*
SO MUCH FOR BEING SYMPATHETIC. SERGEANT REMY -- PREPARE YOUR MEN. WE'RE GOING IN.

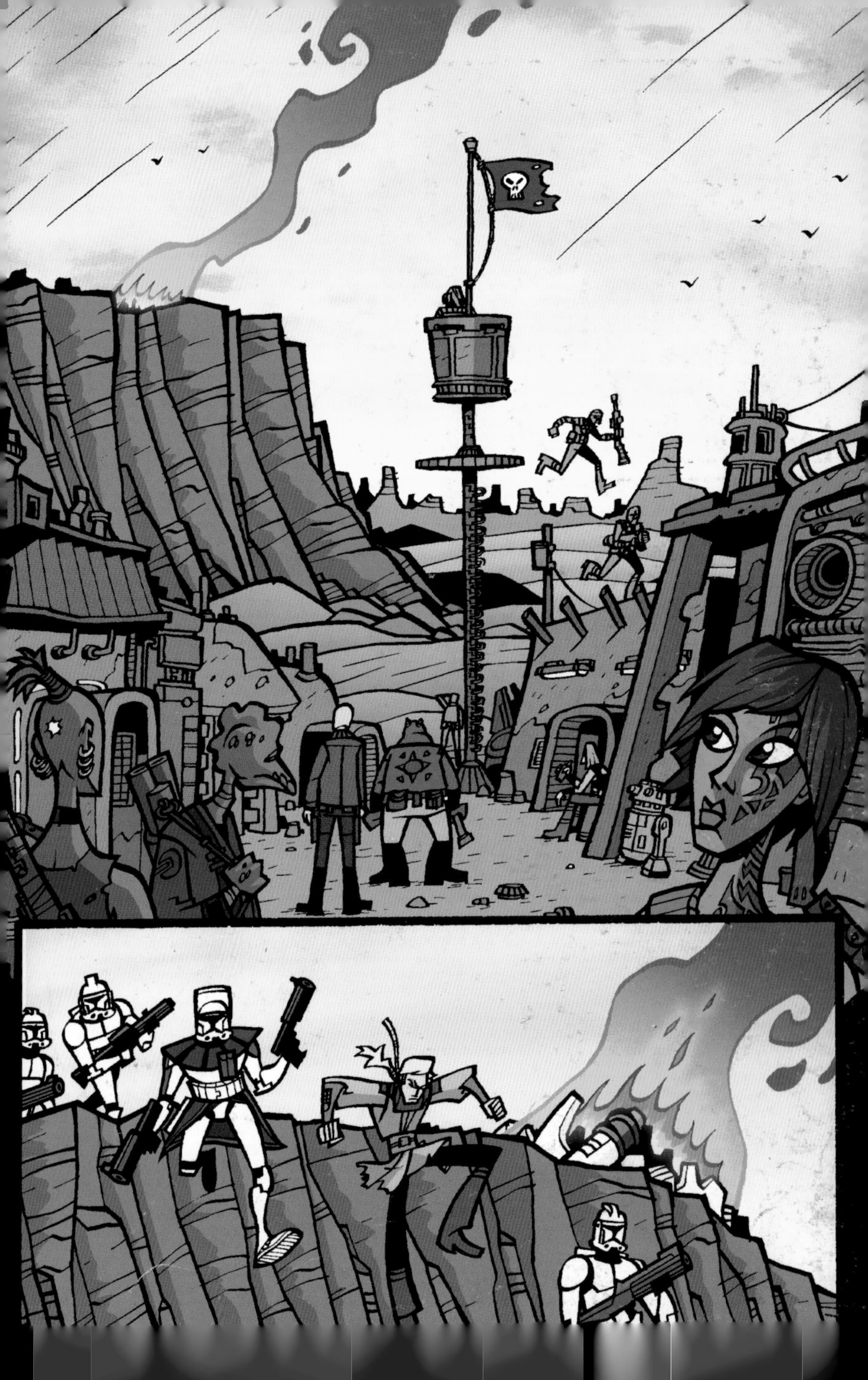

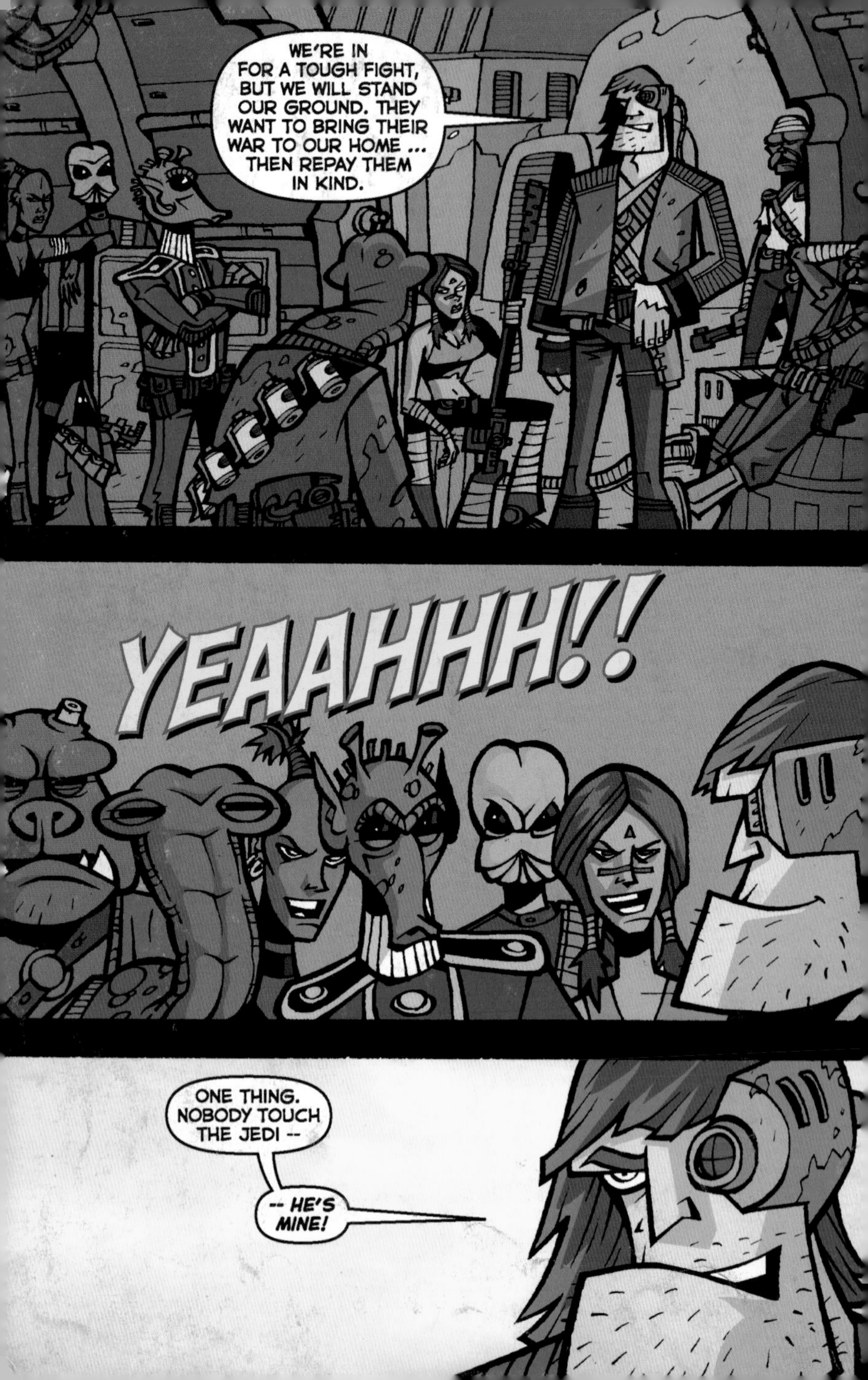
WE'RE IN FOR A TOUGH FIGHT, BUT WE WILL STAND OUR GROUND. THEY WANT TO BRING THEIR WAR TO OUR HOME ... THEN REPAY THEM IN KIND.
YEAAHHH!!
ONE THING. NOBODY TOUCH THE JEDI --
-- HE'S MINE!

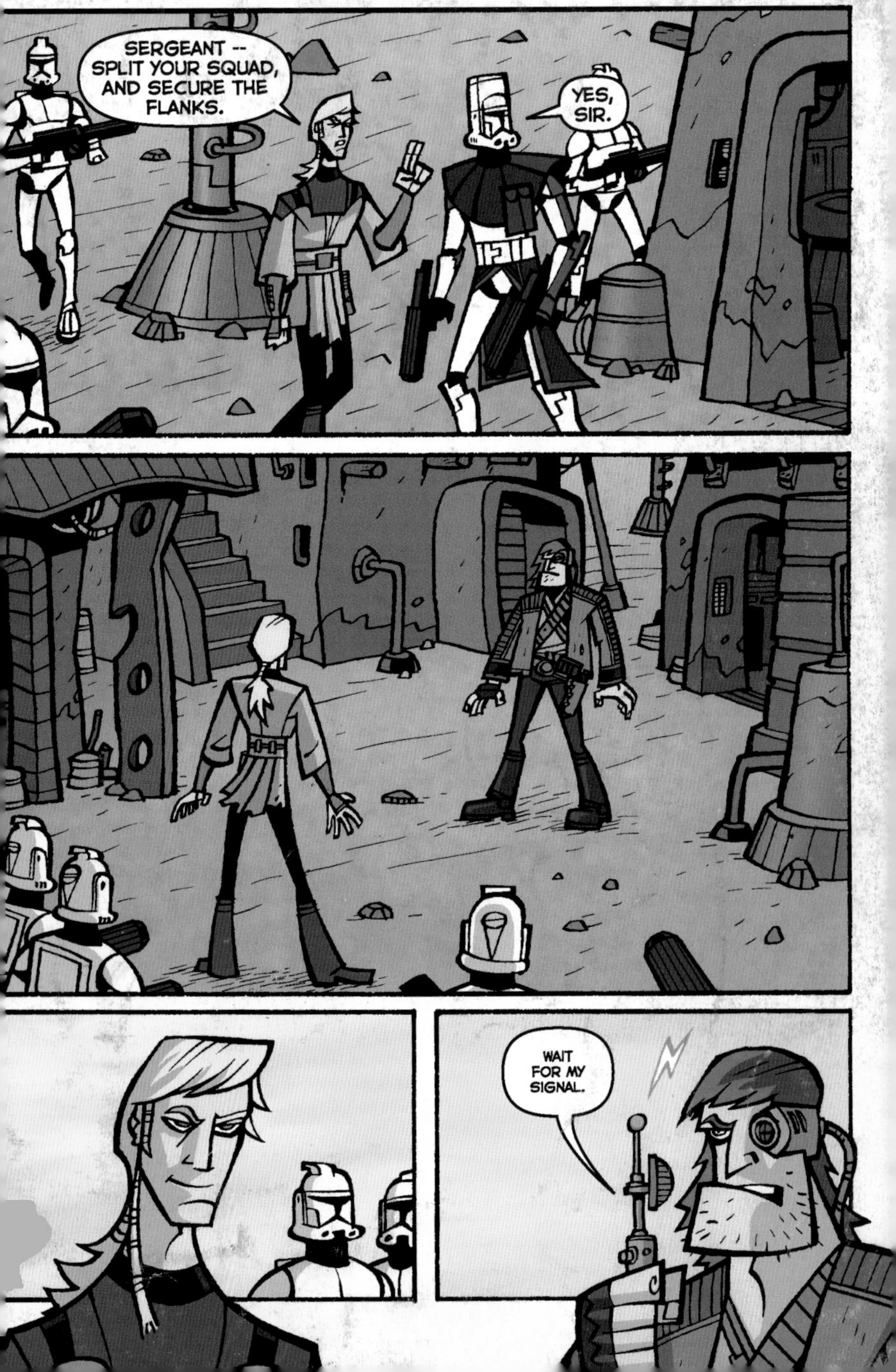
SERGEANT -- SPLIT YOUR SQUAD, AND SECURE THE FLANKS.
YES, SIR.
WAIT FOR MY SIGNAL.

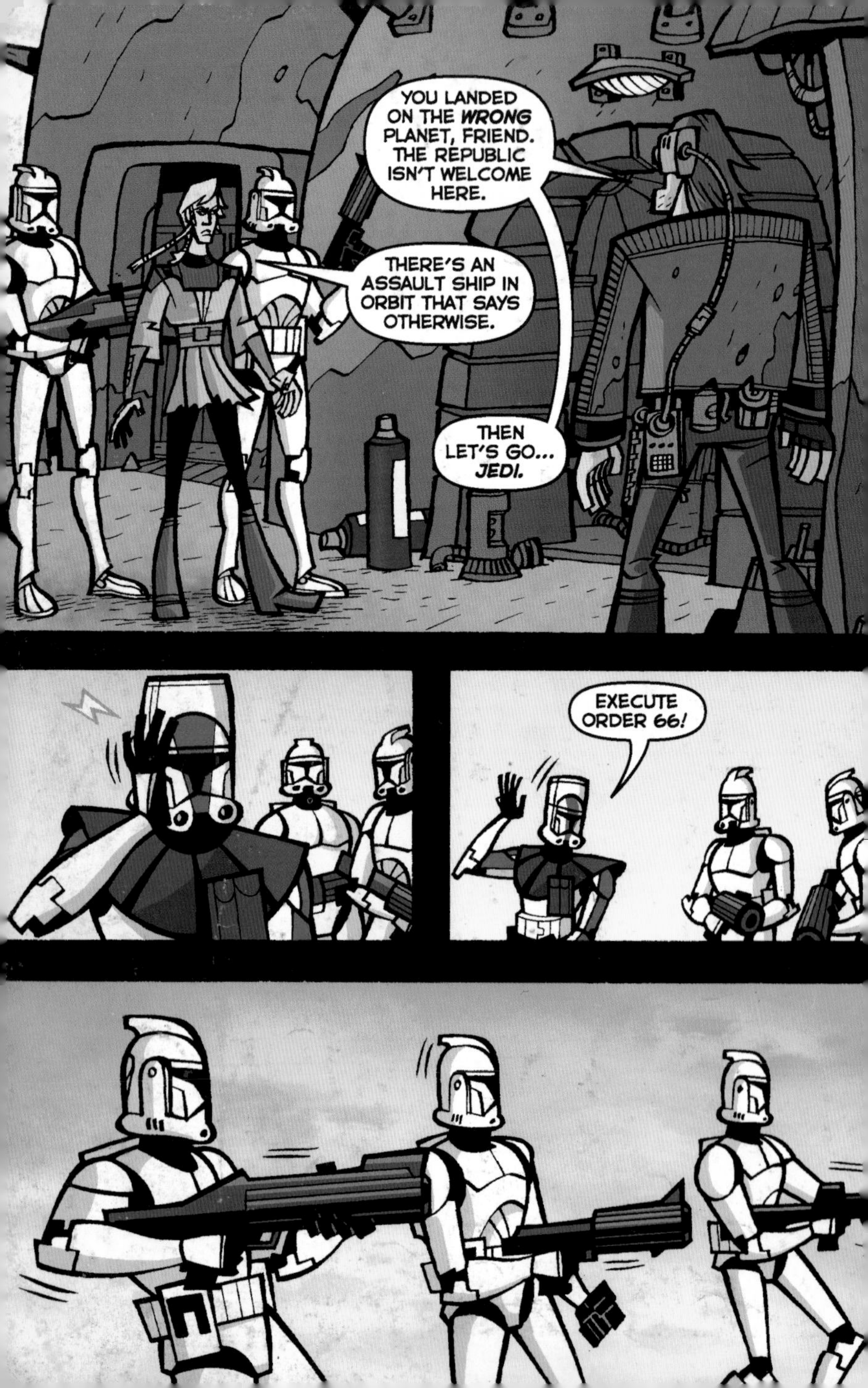
YOU LANDED ON THE *WRONG* PLANET, FRIEND. THE REPUBLIC ISN'T WELCOME HERE.
THERE'S AN ASSAULT SHIP IN ORBIT THAT SAYS OTHERWISE.
THEN LET'S GO... *JEDI.*
EXECUTE ORDER 66!

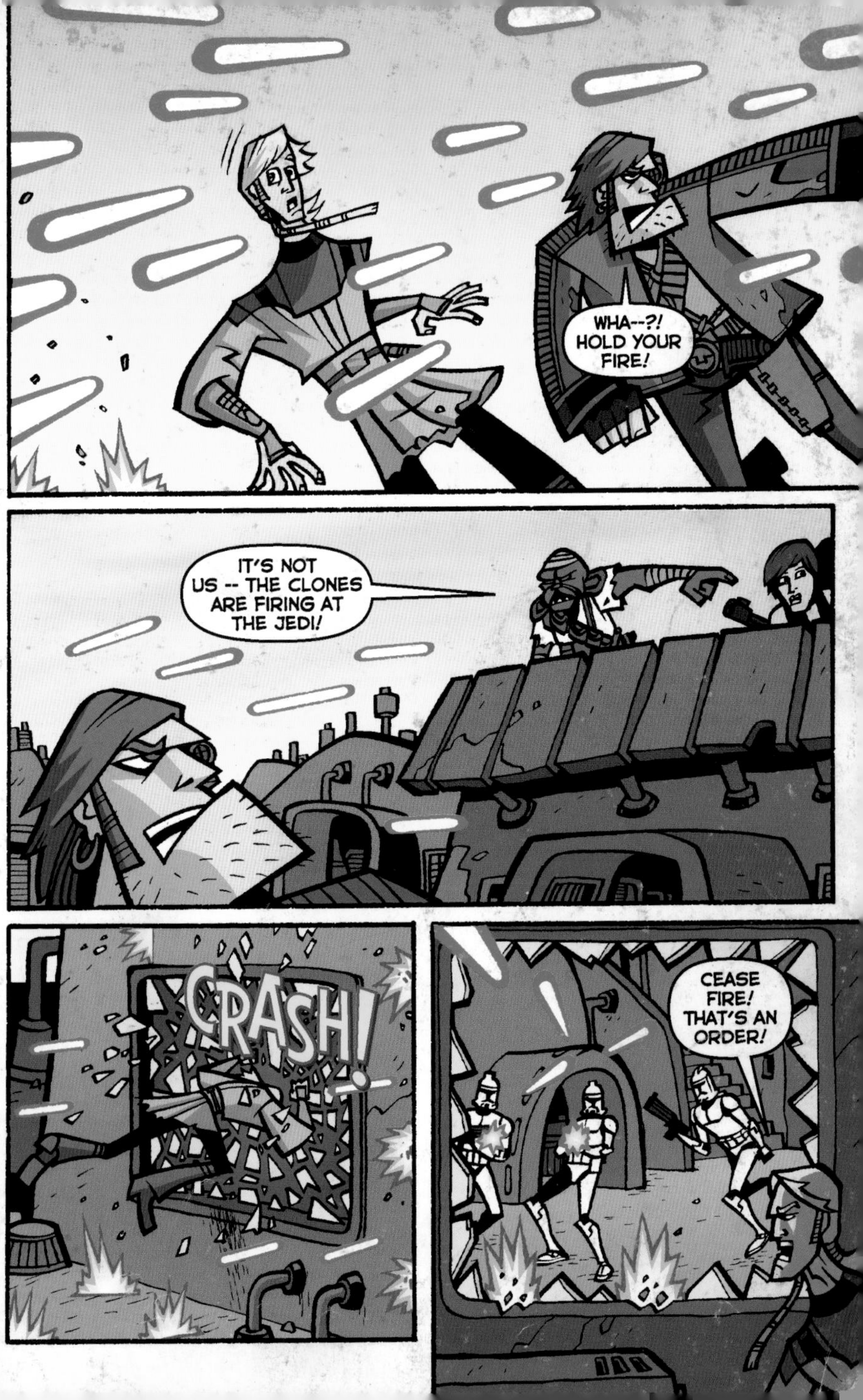
WHA--?! HOLD YOUR FIRE!
IT'S NOT US -- THE CLONES ARE FIRING AT THE JEDI!
CRASH!
CEASE FIRE! THAT'S AN ORDER!

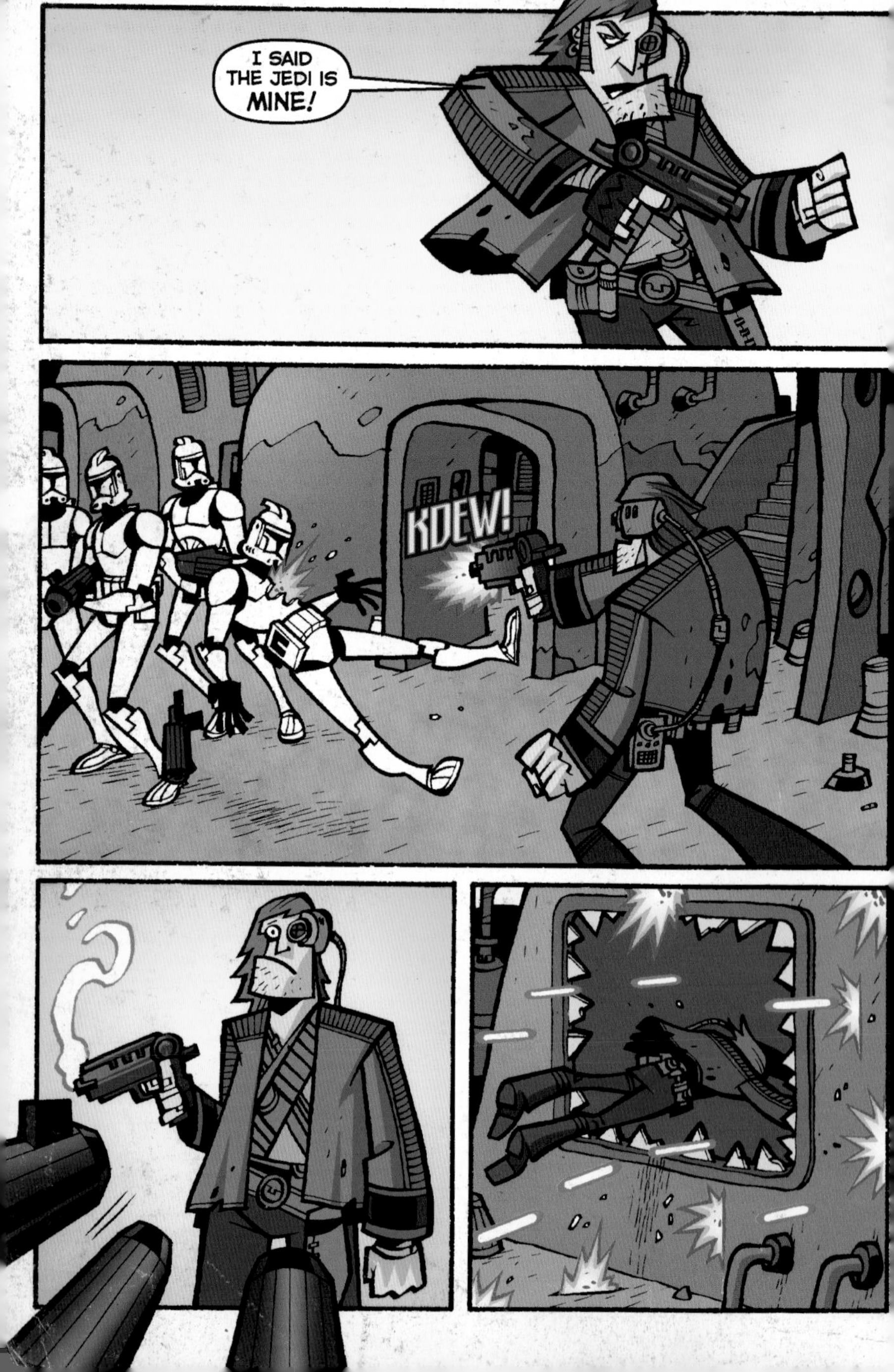
I SAID THE JEDI IS MINE!
KDEW!

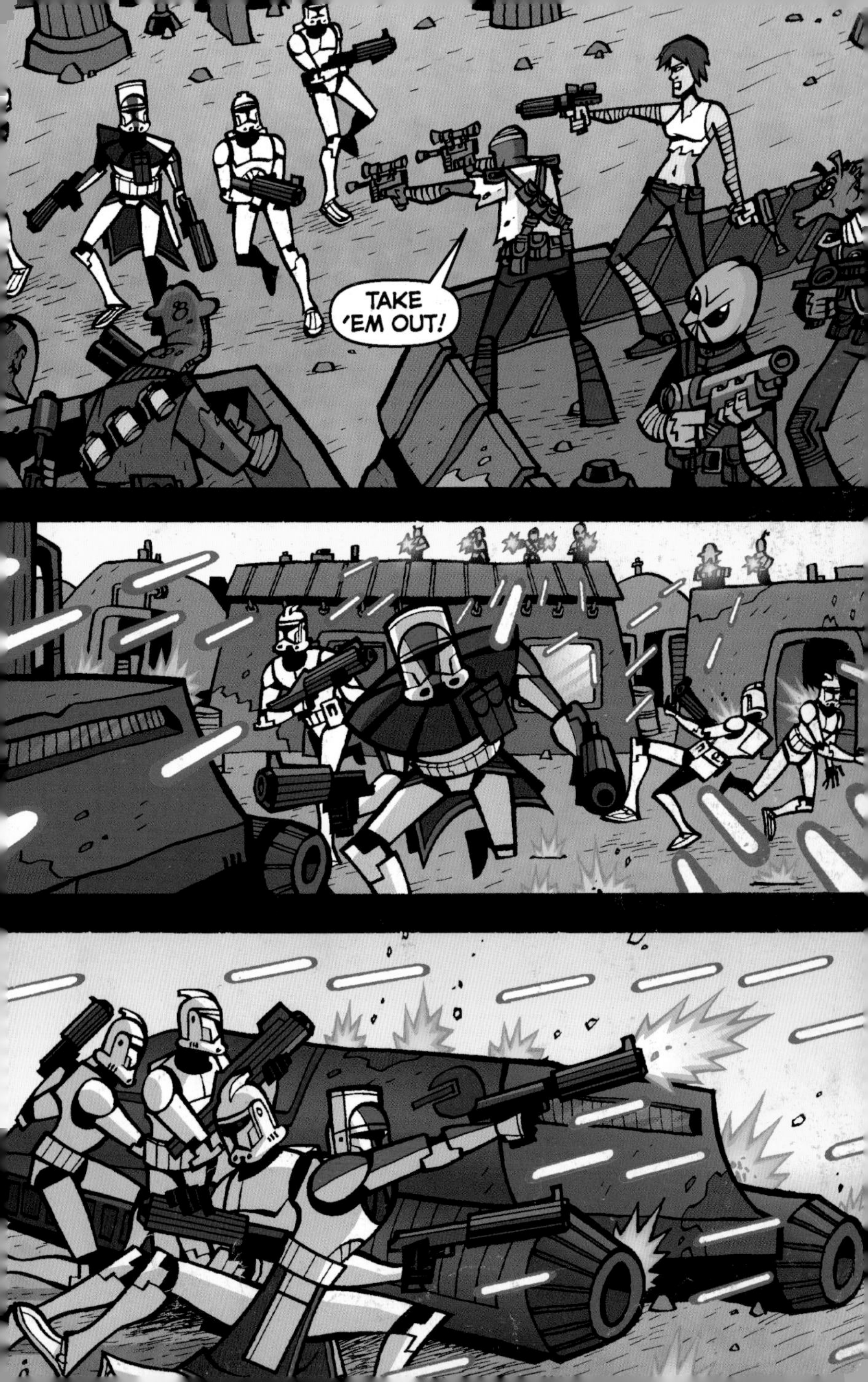
TAKE 'EM OUT!

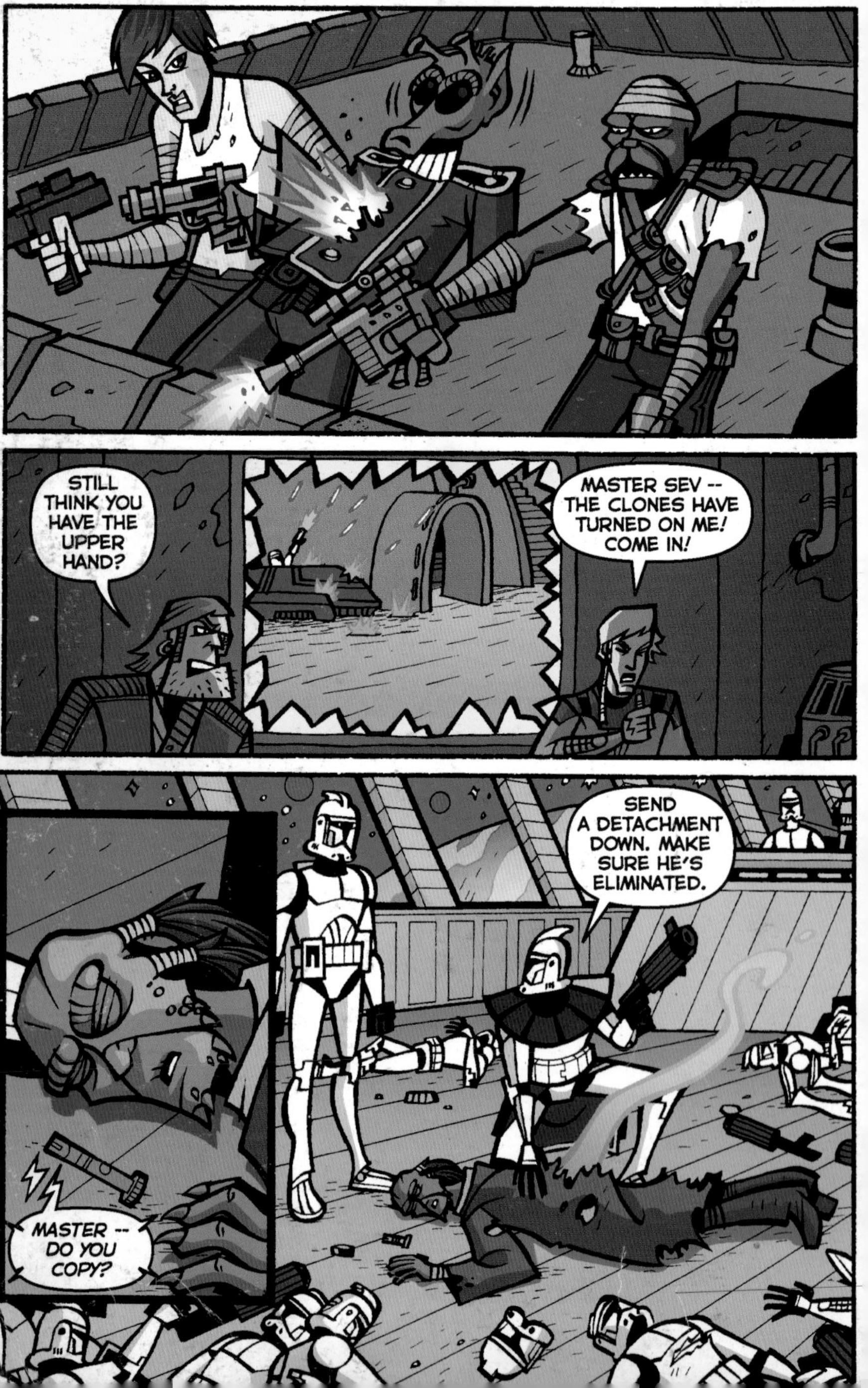
STILL THINK YOU HAVE THE UPPER HAND?
MASTER SEV -- THE CLONES HAVE TURNED ON ME! COME IN!
SEND A DETACHMENT DOWN. MAKE SURE HE'S ELIMINATED.
MASTER -- DO YOU COPY?

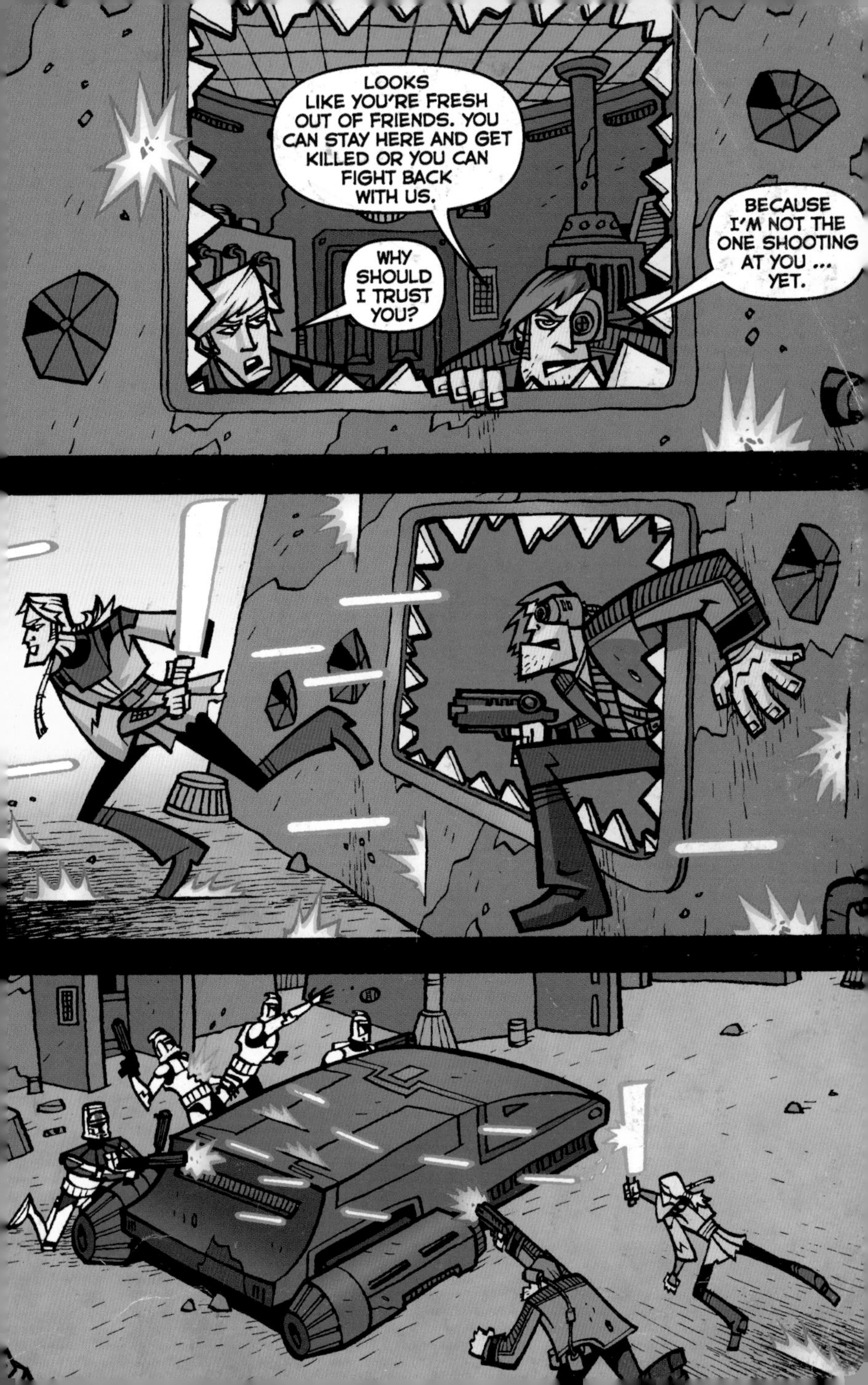
LOOKS LIKE YOU'RE FRESH OUT OF FRIENDS. YOU CAN STAY HERE AND GET KILLED OR YOU CAN FIGHT BACK WITH US.
WHY SHOULD I TRUST YOU?
BECAUSE I'M NOT THE ONE SHOOTING AT YOU ... YET.

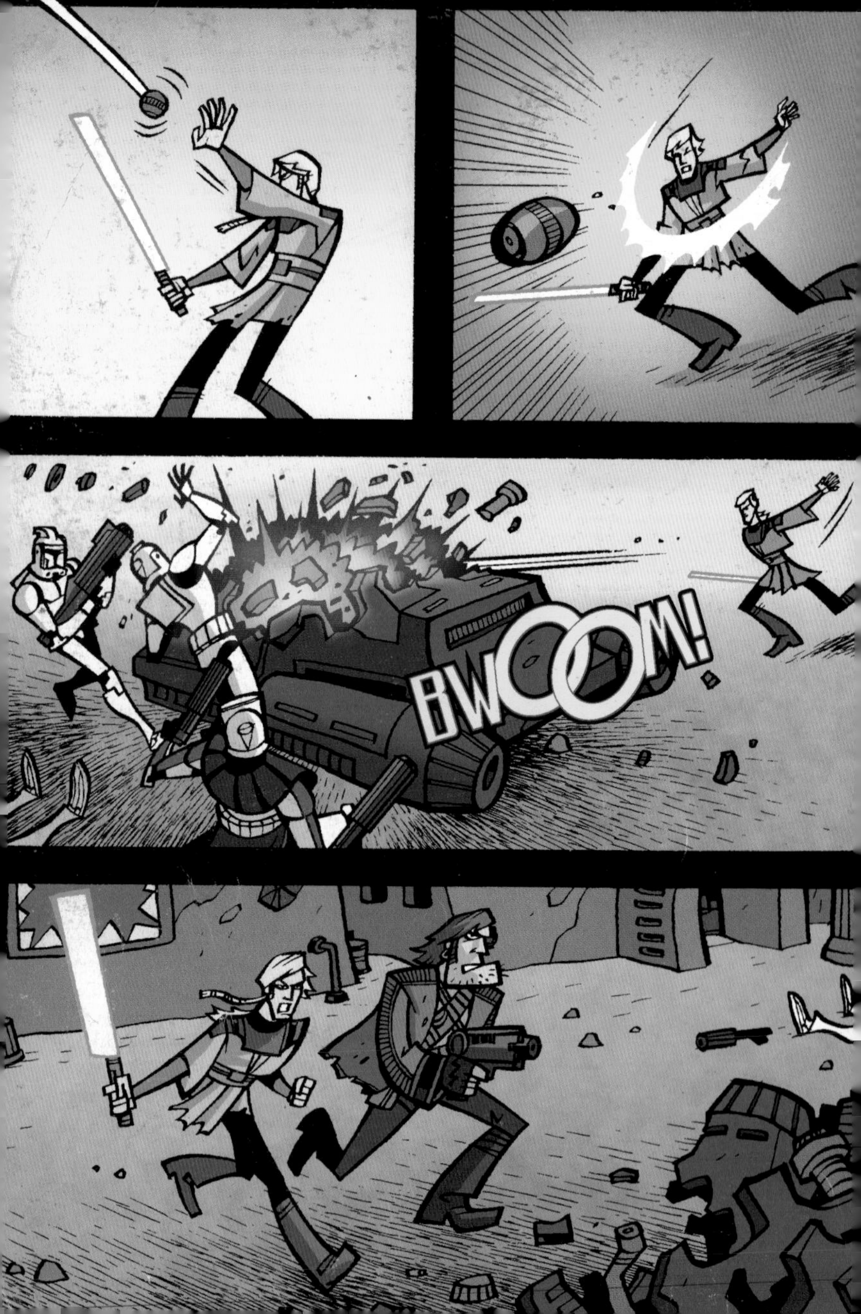
BWOOM!

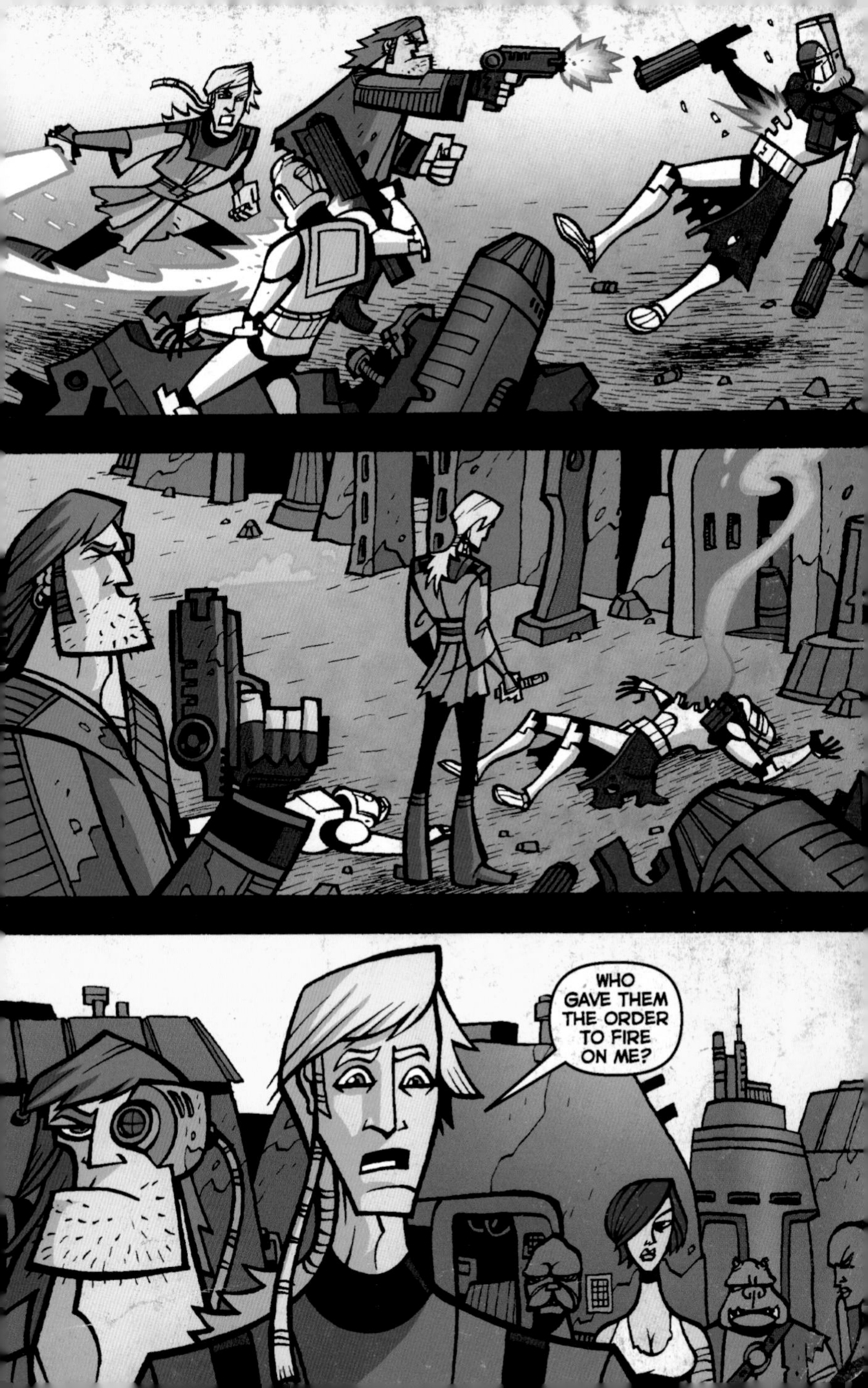
WHO GAVE THEM THE ORDER TO FIRE ON ME?

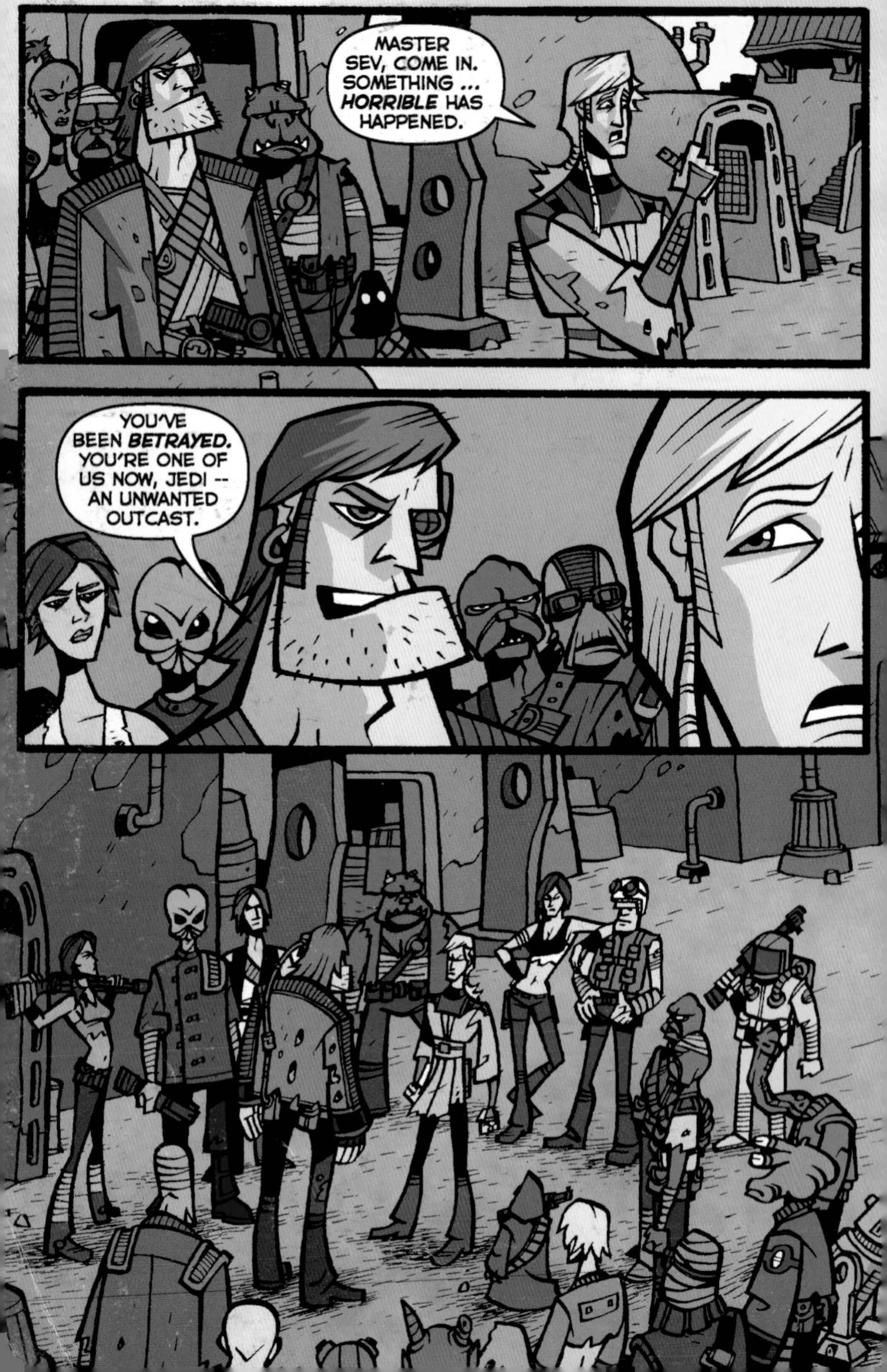
MASTER SEV, COME IN. SOMETHING ... *HORRIBLE* HAS HAPPENED.
YOU'VE BEEN *BETRAYED.* YOU'RE ONE OF US NOW, JEDI -- AN UNWANTED OUTCAST.

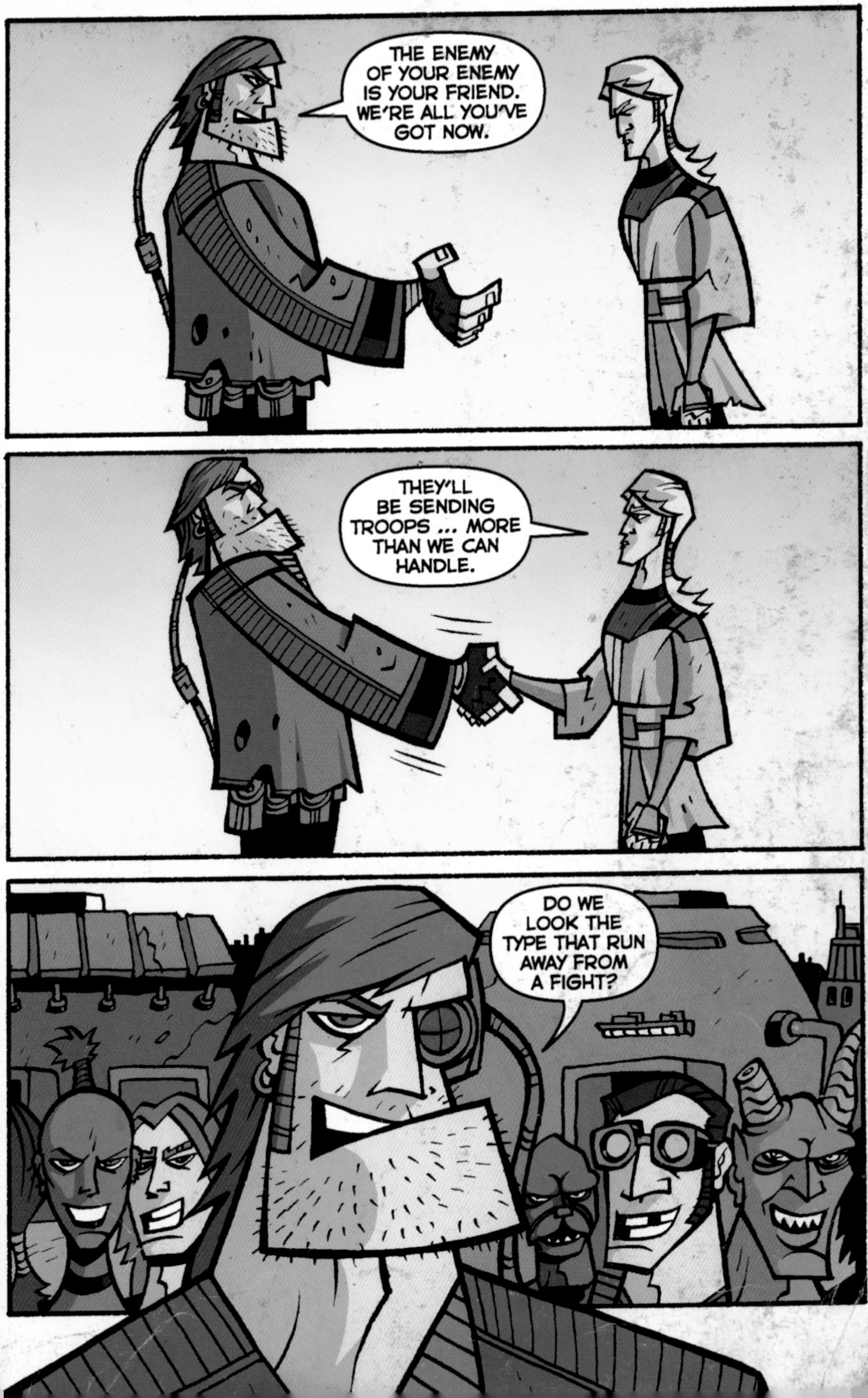
THE ENEMY OF YOUR ENEMY IS YOUR FRIEND. WE'RE ALL YOU'VE GOT NOW.
THEY'LL BE SENDING TROOPS ... MORE THAN WE CAN HANDLE.
DO WE LOOK THE TYPE THAT RUN AWAY FROM A FIGHT?

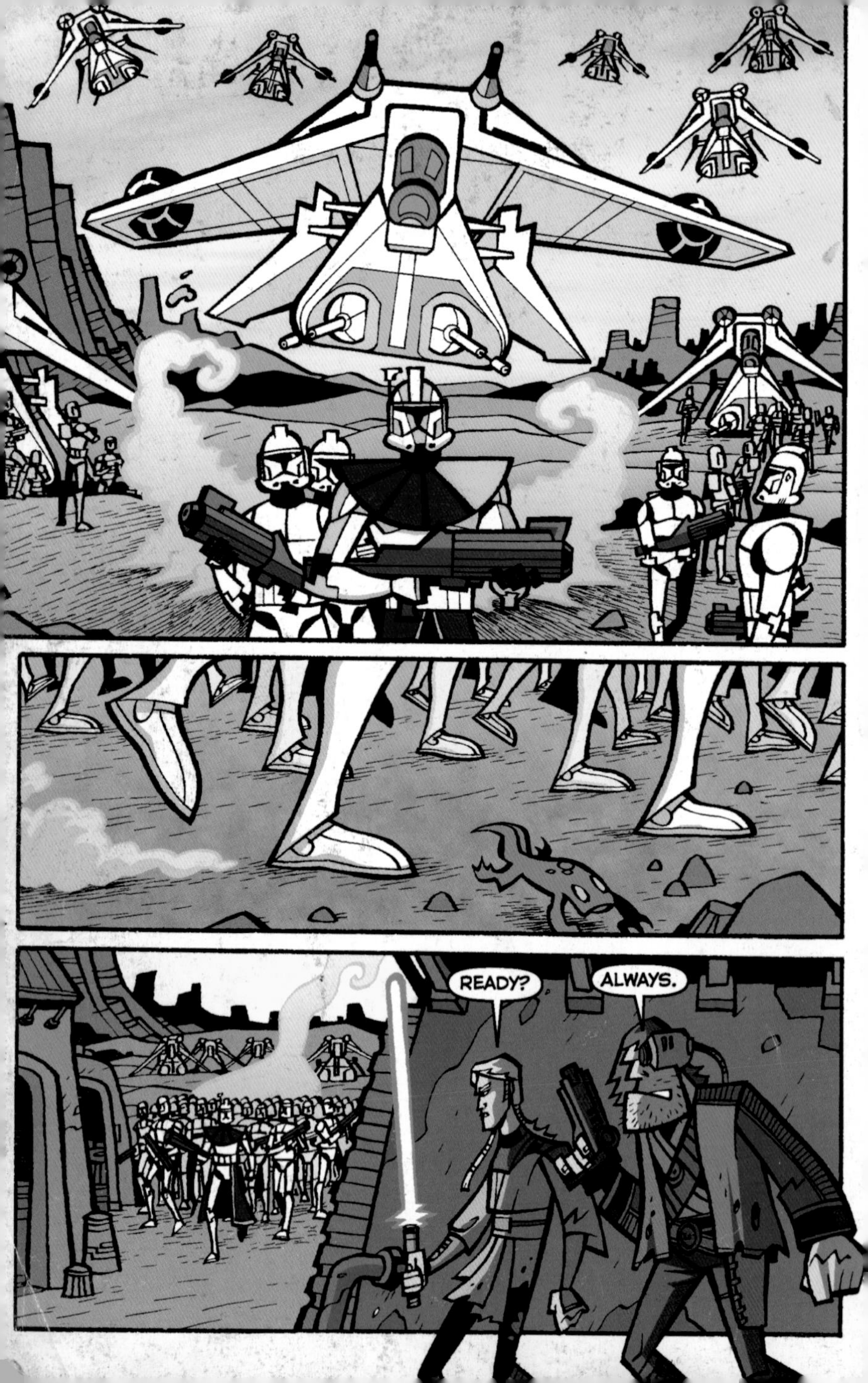
READY?
ALWAYS.

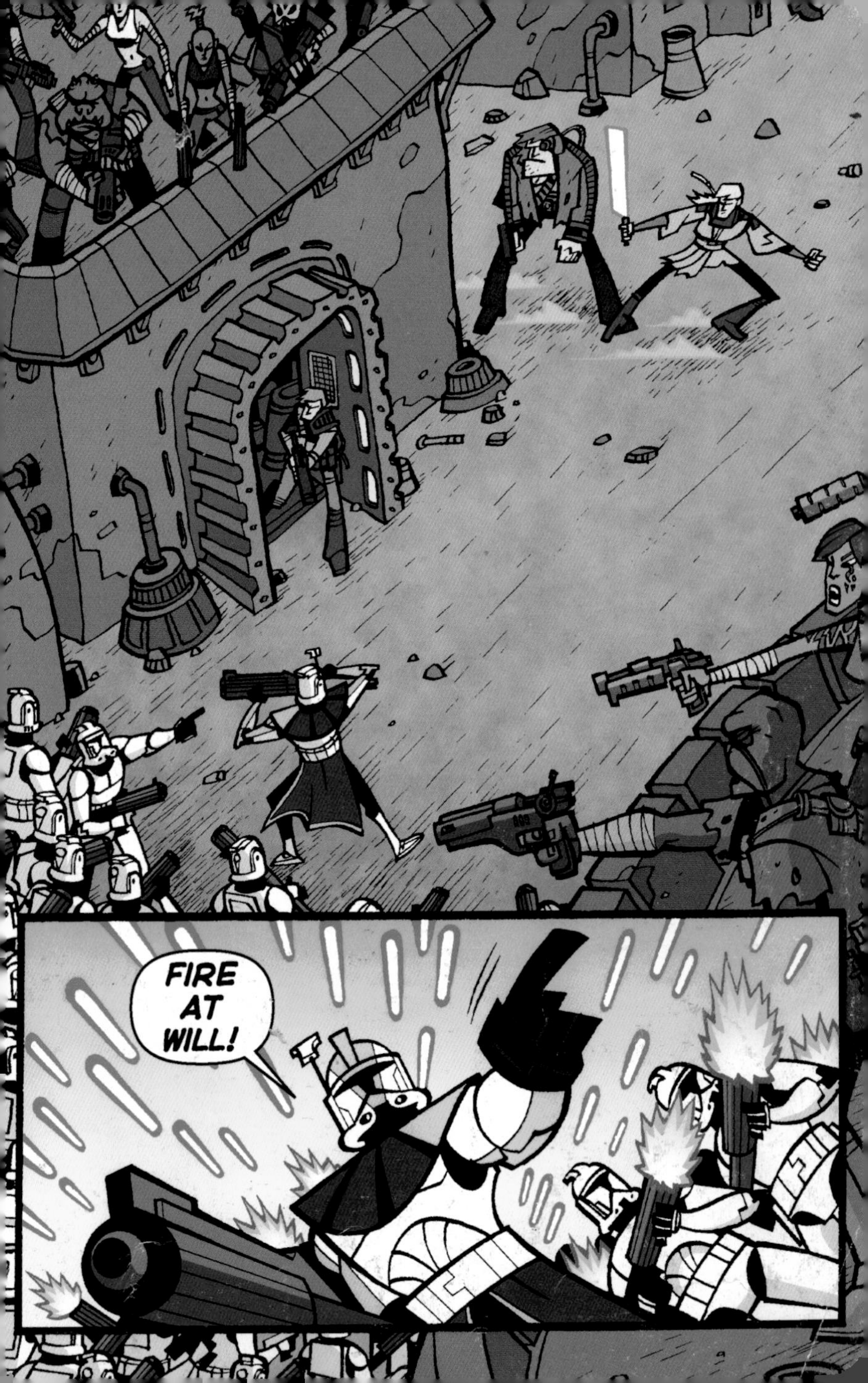
FIRE AT WILL!

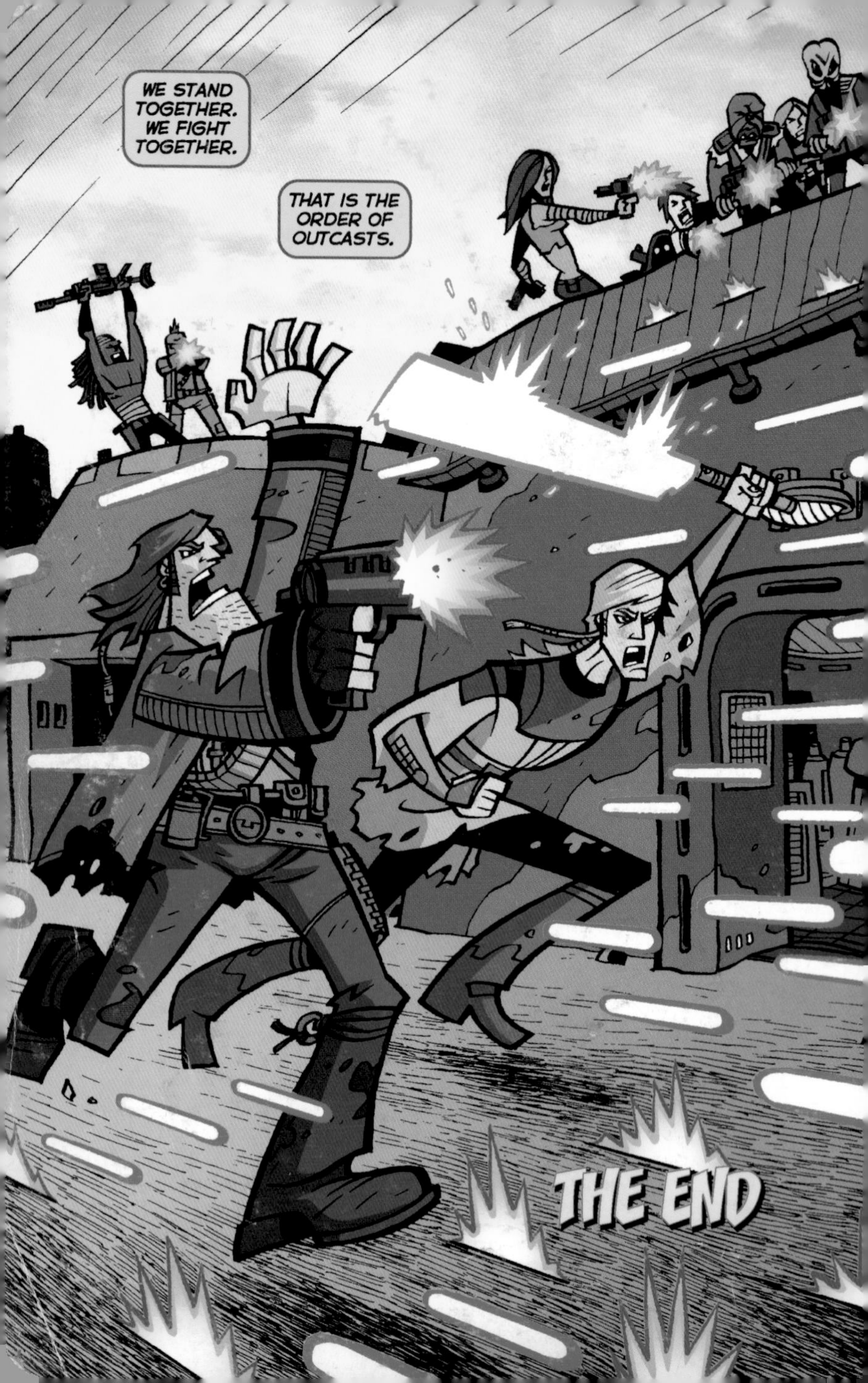
WE STAND TOGETHER. WE FIGHT TOGETHER.
THAT IS THE ORDER OF OUTCASTS.
THE END